# Knitting for Dogs

# IRRESISTIBLE PATTERNS FOR YOUR FAVORITE PUP—AND YOU!

# Knitting for Dogs

sweaters
coats
accessories
and more

*Kristi Porter*

**Photography by Bill Milne**

A FIRESIDE BOOK
Published by Simon & Schuster
New York • London • Toronto • Sydney

FIRESIDE
Rockefeller Center
1230 Avenue of the Americas
New York, NY 10020

FIRESIDE and colophon are registered trademarks
of Simon & Schuster, Inc.

A Quirk Packaging Book
Designed by Lynne Yeamans
Edited by Sarah Scheffel and Elaine Schiebel
Technical editing by Kristi Porter and Mandy Moore
Illustration on page 10 by Erica Mulherin

Manufactured in China

10  9  8  7  6  5  4  3  2  1

Library of Congress Cataloging-in-Publication Data is available

ISBN-13:  978-0-7432-7016-8
ISBN-10:  0-7432-7016-9

For information regarding special discounts for bulk purchases,
please contact Simon & Schuster Special Sales at 1-800-456-6798 or
business@simonandschuster.com

*Outside of a dog, a book is man's best friend.*
*Inside of a dog, it's too dark to read.*
—Groucho Marx

## ACKNOWLEDGMENTS

This book is the work of many hands—and paws. I am lucky to have worked with such a great bunch. My sincere thanks to all of you!

To Amy Swenson, Heather Brack, Kate Watson, and Mandy Moore for working well under pressure and delivering such marvelous patterns.

To Staceyjoy Elkin for putting so much into this book in its earliest days and for providing inspiration to us all.

To the capable folks at Quirk who put the book together: Sharyn Rosart, Sarah Scheffel, Lynne Yeamans, Raina Telgemeier, and Elaine Schiebel.

To those at Simon & Schuster who brought *Knitting for Dogs* into print: Doris Cooper, Lisa Considine, and Sara Schapiro.

To Bill Milne, the photographer, and his staff; his photographs truly bring this book to life.

To the dogs and their owners for modeling our knits—the book wouldn't be the same without you.

To Amy Singer and Kristine Brooks for making good things happen.

To Zoe and Eleanor for their love and patience.

And to Leo, for every reason.

# Contents

# Introduction

Dogs are far more than pets: they've become part of the family, and it's not considered strange to admit it. We sleep in the same room with them (and sometimes in the same bed), take them on vacation with us, and share kisses, food, and toys. We entrust our households and children to their sharp, protective barks and keen territorial instincts.

In return for a place to sleep, a pat on the head, some water and a bowl of chow, we get pure, unconditional love, and lots of it. This collection of fabulous sweaters and irresistible accessories is the perfect opportunity to knit up your gratitude.

Five savvy young designers offer patterns that are for functional, comfortable items—and, let's face it, look really cute. The book opens with great Everyday Sweaters to keep Fido warm and dry, then it's onto Haute Coats, special-occasion coats and ruffles sure to please even the pickiest pups. You and your dog will look smashing in any of the Matchy Matchy sets you choose to knit. And since Accessories Make the Dog, the book closes with a fresh collection of stylish beds, bags, collars, and, of course, toys.

Don't think that sporting dog sweaters is a Small Dogs Only club. These sweaters are designed for dogs of all sizes, from teacup to jumbo. Just take a look at the photographs and you'll see a rollicking assortment of breeds enjoying their knitwear—from big, clumsy retrievers to toy-sized poodles. Tips on measuring your dog and choosing a sweater size will help ensure a good fit, and if sweaters aren't your dog's thing, the accessories ensure he won't be left out in the cold.

Our patterns offer something for knitters of all skill levels. We define a lot of terms and techniques on page 12 and also in the patterns themselves. However, if you come across an unfamiliar technique, any good "how-to" book will steer you right. See the Resources list at the back of the book for suggested reading.

## DOES YOUR DOG NEED A SWEATER?

Dogs from cold climates who spend their days and nights outdoors are naturally insulated against the insults of weather. Their coats are thick and their bodies have enough fat to keep them warm. But what about short-haired house-dogs, bred for warmer weather and accustomed to cushier lives? Sometimes it's an easy call: your mini pinscher probably needs a sweater to keep her from shivering her way through Chicago winters; the neighbor's Siberian husky probably can do without.

These days, most pet dogs (even huskies) do not live outdoors around the clock. They spend much of their time in well-heated homes, so their bodies, naturally enough, acclimate to these cozy indoor environments. When these pets are taken out for cold-weather walks and exercise, the shift to outside temperatures can be a shock to their systems. The solution? Knit up a bulky wool sweater, like the Irish Fisherdog sweater on page 58 (plus some nice matching gloves for yourself). Or arm your pup against the cold with a fleece-lined Houndstooth Hunting Jacket, page 24.

If your beloved dog is getting a little gray around the muzzle, you know that dogs can be senior citizens, too. Older dogs' bodies are sensitive to the cold, so do something nice for yours and knit him a soft, warm sweater or jacket. Legwarmers (see page 89) might be just the thing for an older dog suffering from stiff joints and arthritis.

Let's not forget those dogs that love wearing clothes. Aside from the warmth of an additional layer or two, they revel in the attention they receive for their snappy knitwear and may really strut their stuff. If you own one of these show-dog wannabes (or a real show dog!), consider knitting her a whole wardrobe of dog clothes, from everyday sweaters to sparkles and faux fur. (The Haute Coats chapter offers projects that'd be perfect for her.) You care about what you wear. Why shouldn't your best pal be as warm and stylishly dressed as you are?

## WHICH YARN SHOULD YOU USE?

The patterns call for yarns that will yield great results—and look smashing, too. If you want to try a different yarn though, feel free to substitute. For all projects where it matters, gauge is given in stitches and rows per four inches. In your search for alternatives, look for yarns with a similar gauge. Of course, even yarns of the same gauge can vary widely—a silk yarn will look and behave differently from a mohair one. A yarn with a texture similar to the one suggested will yield the best results, but if you have the time to experiment, go ahead! Unless you own a jumbo-sized dog, these sweaters are relatively small, so experiment away. But don't forget, when you've substituted yarns, it's especially important to make a gauge swatch.

Many of the patterns in this book are knit in natural fibers. They insulate well and breathe better than synthetics, so your doggy will feel cozy but not claustrophobic. Furthermore, wool stays warm even when wet; a synthetic yarn will not. If you can't stand the idea of hand washing, an acrylic blend or superwash wool may be the way to go because they can be machine washed with no ill effects. Most likely, you want to knit a functional sweater for your dog, not a museum piece, so choose yarns that match the amount of care you care to give.

## HOW TO CHOOSE THE RIGHT SIZE FOR YOUR DOG

The best way to determine what size sweater is appropriate for your dog is by chest measurement. When your dog is calm and standing still, measure around his chest at its widest point. Do not pull the tape measure tightly; allow it to sit comfortably around the dog's chest. Next measure the length of your dog's back. With the dog standing and looking straight ahead, measure from the collar to the base (not tip!) of the tail. If your dog is skittish or too curious about the tape measure to stand still, enlist a helper to distract him while you measure.

Use the chart on the next page to determine the size that most closely matches your dog's chest measurement, allowing for a bit of ease—as little as half an inch for tiny dogs, up to four inches for the largest dogs. Our patterns will fit dogs with chest measurements from 8 to 36 inches, though not every pattern includes directions for the full size range. (What looks good on a Yorkie is unlikely to suit a rottweiler!)

## HE JUST WON'T WEAR IT (*or* Sweater-Haters' Anonymous)

Sure, you'll encounter dogs who are not comfortable in sweaters; like the love of a particular chew toy, it's a matter of personal preference. If your dog has never worn a sweater, here's a way to tell if he will tolerate a sweater without going to the trouble of knitting one: Put him in a child-sized T-shirt with the sleeves cut off and see how he reacts. Don't try this when it's 95° and make sure that the shirt is not too big or too small. If the dog ignores it or starts strutting around, you've got an ideal candidate for a dog sweater. If the dog panics, tries to bite or scratch it off, refuses to move, or exhibits other visibly unhappy behavior, take it off immediately.

But don't give up yet! Try again a few days later, leaving the T-shirt on for 15-minute intervals to see if he warms to the idea. If he does, you can feel confident he will appreciate a sweater, so cast on without fear. If not, do not insist he wear one. You and the animal will both get stressed out, and it's not worth it. Instead, turn to Accessories Make the Dog, and try one of the hand-knit collar patterns. Even a dog who won't wear a sweater will enjoy a fun new toy or a cozy dog bed knit with love by their favorite human!

## CUSTOMIZE THE FIT

It is generally easier to adjust the length of the sweater than the width, so remember to always choose your size based on the chest measurement. If your dog's back length measurement is significantly longer or shorter than the length specified in the pattern, you will want to modify the pattern for a good fit. A skinny dog like a greyhound may need his sweater lengthened; a particularly barrel-chested bull dog will likely need her sweater shortened. It's worth the extra effort: you'll be happier with the final results and so will your pooch.

You should add or subtract the appropriate number of inches to the back panel behind the leg holes. Alter the front panel by the same amount. Any shaping done on these pieces should be worked as specified in the pattern. Start with the diagrams that accompany the pattern to figure out the adjusted measurements for your customized sweater.

## SWEATER SIZING CHART

Use this chart to determine the sweater size that's right for your dog. Start with her chest measurement to determine size; check length to determine whether you need to shorten or lengthen the sweater pattern to fit your dog.

The last column lists a few of the breeds that would typically wear each sweater size. However, matching breed to size is not a perfect science. The typical bull terrier would wear a medium; yours might require a small. A standard dachshund and a pug both wear XS sweaters, but the dachshund's sweater would need to be lengthened. Each dog is unique; be sure to measure your pup before deciding on a size.

| size | dog's girth | dog's length (from collar to tailbone) | sweater girth | sweater length | typical breed |
|------|-------------|----------------------------------------|---------------|----------------|---------------|
| XXS | 7" to 10" | 10" | 10" | 8" | Yorkie, Chihuahua, Toy Poodle |
| XS | 10" to 13" | 14" | 14" | 12" | Pug, Dachshund, Pekingese |
| S | 13" to 17" | 18" | 18" | 16" | Cocker Spaniel, Corgi, Lhasa Apso |
| M | 17" to 21" | 22" | 22" | 20" | Beagle, Whippet, Bulldog |
| L | 21" to 25" | 26" | 26" | 24" | Standard Poodle, Labrador, Greyhound |
| XL | 25" to 29" | 30" | 30" | 28" | Collie, German Shepherd, Chow Chow |
| XXL | 29" to 33" | 32" | 34" | 30" | Rottweiler, Doberman, Akita |
| XXXL | 33" to 37" | 34" | 38" | 32" | Bullmastiff, Short-haired St. Bernard |

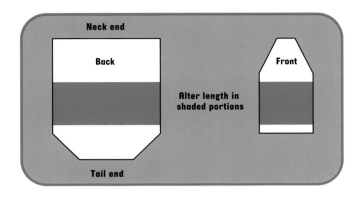

## HOW TO PUT A SWEATER ON A DOG

It's in your dog's best interest for you to learn to do this quickly. Scrunch the sweater up like a sock and put your dog's head through the neck hole. Put your hand through a leg opening (from the outside of the sweater) and grasp her foot, covering the nails with your hand, then gently lead the foot through the leg opening. Repeat for the other leg. The idea is to prevent the delicate toes, especially the dewclaws, if your dog has them, from getting tangled in the knit fabric. That hurts!

We have found that many dogs who are happy enough wearing sweaters do not like sleeves. Therefore, all the patterns in this book can be knit without sleeves, though some have optional directions for them. Knit sleeves if you like, but be forewarned that even good-natured dogs may not like them.

With one exception, harness or collar openings are not built into these patterns because the exact spot that's comfortable for your pet is different for each animal. Harnesses should go underneath the sweaters, not over them. After the sweater is on your dog, find the metal loop on the collar or harness and hook on the leash through the sweater. After a few wearings, the knitting will naturally begin to part at that spot, and you can go back and blanket stitch or crochet around that area to make a permanent opening if you'd like. (See Everyday Turtleneck, page 17, for more specific instructions on knitting a leash opening into the sweater.)

## CARING FOR DOG SWEATERS

You may not need to clean your own sweaters very often. But you don't gallop through puddles, dig in garbage cans, or mark every fire hydrant that crosses your path. Dogs are harder on their sweaters, so you'll need to wash them more frequently. Dogs can stink, but their sweaters need not!

Hand wash or dry clean your dog's hand knits at least once or twice a year (or whenever they look or smell like they need it!), and always clean them at the end of the cold season before you pack them away. Wash garments according to the care needs specified on the yarn's ball band; the patterns in this book also offer tips on special care. If in doubt, a sure approach is to hand wash the sweater with a gentle shampoo or dishwashing liquid in a lukewarm bath in the sink. Immerse and let soak for 15 minutes; drain and repeat for especially dirty or smelly items. Rinse two or three times in lukewarm water to get the soap out. Roll the sweater in a towel and squeeze to remove excess moisture, then lay flat to dry. You may need to turn the sweater inside out to thoroughly dry both sides. Never put a damp sweater on your pooch! While hand washing your dog's sweater may seem like an extra burden, take cheer that at least the sweater will not shake itself dry in the middle of your living room!

## ABBREVIATIONS AND TECHNIQUES

This book assumes a familiarity with basic knitting terms and techniques. If a technique is new to you and you want to learn more about it, see book recommendations and online resources on page 95.

**BO** Bind off stitches

**Cable cast on** Also called *knitted cast on.*

**CC** Contrast color

**Dec** Decrease

**Decrease bind-off** [K2tog, sl stitch back to left needle] Repeat to end of row.

**DK** Double knit, double knitting. This technique creates a doubled fabric with two right sides—and an opening between them. On an even number of stitches, work all rows: [K1, sl 1 wyib] to end of row.

**DPNs** Double-pointed needles. Useful for working in the round, especially in tight places.

**g** Grams

**Icord** Makes a thin tube. On double-pointed needles, knit across prescribed number of stitches, but do not turn work. Slide stitches to other end of needle and knit again over same stitches, being careful to pull yarn snugly across back of work between rows. Repeat until cord reaches desired length.

**K** Knit

**K1fb** Knit into the front and back of next stitch. Also called a "bar increase."

**K2tog** Knit two stitches together (a right-leaning decrease).

**M1** Make one stitch. Pick up the horizontal bar between two stitches and knit through its back loop (an increase).

**Mattress Stitch** A technique used to seam pieces almost invisibly. Use a yarn needle and thread to sew the two pieces, working on the "ladders" between the first and second stitches on each piece. Work from the right side of piece.

**MC** Main color

**mm** Millimeters

**P** Purl

**P2tog** Purl two stitches together (a decrease)

**PSSO** Pass slipped stitch(es) over

**Reverse Stockinette Stitch** Stockinette Stitch with the purl side as the right side of the work.

**RS** Right (public) side of work

**Seed Stitch** For an even number of stitches, [k1, p1] across. On second row, [p1, k1] across. Knit the purl stitches and purl the knit stitches.

**Sl** Slip

**Sl 1** Slip one stitch. Slip the stitch purlwise unless otherwise indicated.

**Sl 1 wyib** Slip one stitch purlwise with yarn in back.

**Sl 1 wyif** Slip one stitch purlwise with yarn in front.

**Sl 1, k2tog, psso** Slip one stitch, knit two stitches together, pass the slipped stitch over the completed k2tog (a double decrease)

**SSK** Slip two stitches knitwise, one at a time, then stick left needle through the fronts of these two stitches from left to right and knit the two together (a left-leaning decrease).

**St(s)** Stitch(es)

**Tog** Together

**W+T** Wrap next stitch and turn. A technique used to create tidy rows.

**WS** Wrong side of work

**wyib** With yarn in back

**wyif** With yarn in front

**yd(s)** Yard(s)

**YO** Yarn over, or yarn forward. Bring yarn to front between stitches. Work next stitch. A yarn over creates an eyelet and an increase.

**\*...\* or [...]** Repeat directions between asterisks or brackets as indicated in pattern.

# Everyday Sweaters

A walk in the park, a trip to the grocery store, a playdate with his best pal—make the mundane out of the ordinary with these fun, fresh designs. Maybe he needs a Houndstooth Hunting Jacket, lined with fleece for extra warmth, or a Nightwalker Sport Coat, which features glow-in-the-dark stripes for late-night jaunts. This collection of hardworking sweaters will help keep your pooch warm and cozy through whatever weather (or adventures!) come his way.

* **Essential Puppy Pullover**
* **Everyday Turtleneck**
* **Nightwalker Sport Coat**
* **Houndstooth Hunting Jacket**
* **Rain-Resistant Coat and Hoodie**
* **Raglan Monogrammed Sweater**

# Essential Puppy Pullover
*Designed by Staceyjoy Elkin, Pattern by Kristi Porter*

**If you were to knit just one sweater for your dog, this garden-variety garter-stitch pullover would be a good choice. Flattering on any dog, this sweater is so soft and comfortable, your pup may forget she's wearing it. Better still, it's a cinch to make, even for beginners.**

## MATERIALS

* Manos del Uruguay Wool (100% wool; 138 yds per 100g skein):
    [MC] Color: 51 Jade; 1(2, 2, 3, 4) skeins
    [CC] Color: 114 Bramble (or other contrasting color); less than 1 skein is used for optional belly band.

* 1 set US 9/5.5 mm needles
    (or size needed to match gauge)

## GAUGE

14 stitches/28 rows = 4 inches in Garter Stitch (to find an appropriate substitute yarn, look for one with a recommended gauge of 16 stitches/20 rows = 4 inches in Stockinette Stitch)

## SIZE

**Sweater chest measurement:** 14(18, 22, 26, 30) inches
**Finished length:** 10(14, 16, 18, 20) inches

## SWEATER

### Back

The back is a simple rectangle, knit from neck to tail.

With MC, cast on 34(46, 54, 62, 74) stitches. [K2, p2] across, end k2. Work in k2, p2 rib as established until piece measures 2(2, 2, 3, 3) inches.

Switch to Garter Stitch and work without shaping until piece measures 9(13, 15, 17, 19) inches. Return to k2, p2 rib and work 1 inch. Back should now measure 10(14, 16, 18, 20) inches. Bind off loosely in rib.

## Belly Panel

(Omit if your boy tends to wet his sweater!)

With CC, cast on 14(18, 24, 28, 32) stitches.
Row 1: [K1, p1] across.
Row 2: [P1, k1] across.
Continue in Seed Stitch as established (repeating Rows 1 and 2) for 2 inches. Proceed to front.

## Front

The front is knit from belly to neck.

Cast on 14(18, 24, 28, 32) stitches with MC.

Work in Garter Stitch until piece measures 2(5, 6, 7, 8) inches from beginning of Garter Stitch.

Next row (right side): K5(7, 10, 12, 14) stitches, k2tog, place marker, k2tog, k5(7, 10, 12, 14) stitches.

Continue decreasing 1 stitch on either side of marker on every right-side row until 2 stitches remain. Bind off.

**FINISHING**

To create the ribbed neck, fold the back in half lengthwise and seam together the two sides along the longer ribbed section (the cast on end) of the piece.

Place the point of the front at the V just below the ribbed collar you have seamed. Seam about an inch on either side of the point. A fitting on your dog now will help you determine the size and position of the armholes. Seam Front to Back on either side from the cast on edge of the Front to just behind the forelegs.

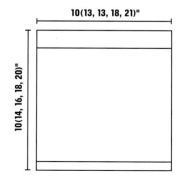

10(13, 13, 18, 21)"

10(14, 16, 18, 20)"

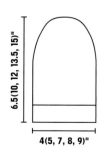

6.5(10, 12, 13.5, 15)"

4(5, 7, 8, 9)"

# Everyday Turtleneck  *By Heather Brack*

A busy day of chasing cats, tennis balls, and his tail is no reason for your puppy not to dress his best. This turtleneck is knit from colorful but tough wool that will stand up to some abuse and stay warm even when damp. Its belly-baring design means there's less fabric to snag or tangle during play. A little buttonhole in the back of the turtleneck means it's leash compatible. For tips on how to wash this hardworking sweater, see Caring for Dog Sweaters, page 11.

## MATERIALS

* Noro Kureyon (100% wool; 110 yds per 50g skein); Color: 52; 1(2, 3, 5, 6) skeins
* 1 set US 9/5.5 mm needles
* 1 set US 9/5.5 mm DPNs (or size needed to match gauge)

## GAUGE

18 stitches/24 rows = 4 inches in Stockinette Stitch

## SIZE

**Dog's chest measurement:** 10(14, 18, 22, 26) inches
**Finished length:** 5(9, 13, 17, 21) inches from base of neck to end.

(This sweater is designed to end 3 to 5 inches from your dog's tail. Feel free to customize the length to suit a dog with a longer or shorter back, but make sure to buy extra yarn if you plan on lengthening the sweater.)

## SWEATER

Cast on 36(54, 72, 90, 108) stitches. Work back and forth across all stitches in k2, p2 rib for 4(5, 7, 9, 11) inches.

Knit 1 row.
Purl 1 row.

### Optional leash opening

K16(25, 34, 43, 52), bind off 4 stitches, k16(25, 34, 43, 52).
P16(25, 34, 43, 52), cast on 4 stitches using cable cast on, p16(25, 34, 43, 52).

K1, k1fb, k to last 3 stitches, k1fb, k2.
Purl 1 row.
Repeat last 2 rows 6 more times. 50(68, 86, 104, 122) stitches on needles.

Work even in Stockinette Stitch for 1(1.5, 2, 3, 3.5) inches.

### Sleeve openings

Row 1: on RS row, k5(7, 9, 11, 13),
Bind off 7(9, 11, 13, 15) stitches, k26(36, 46, 56, 66),
Bind off 7(9, 11, 13, 15) stitches, k5(7, 9, 11, 13).

Row 2: Begin the sleeve steeks.
P5(7, 9, 11, 13), cast on 4 stitches, k to bound off stitches, cast on 4 stitches, purl to end of row.
Work in Stockinette Stitch for 1(2, 2.5, 3, 3.5) inches.

## WHAT'S STEEKING?

Steeking is a technique traditionally used in Fair Isle sweaters to minimize the number of ends that need to be woven in and to allow knitters to work in the round even at armholes. Instead of breaking the yarn and knitting on either side of the opening, four to eight new stitches are cast on and then cut apart when the sleeves and neckband are attached.

In this sweater, steeking across the leg holes allows the stripes in the yarn to continue unbroken. Instead of knitting around each leg hole, you're going to bind off the edge, then cast on a few extra stitches in the next row and knit straight across the opening. When you finish knitting, you cut the steek open. Don't worry, the wool will stick to itself until you can sew the cut edges down on the inside. And the pattern will guide you through the process, step by step.

On next RS row: K5(7, 9, 11, 13), BO 4 stitches, k to steek, bind off 4 stitches, knit to end of row.

### Close the sleeve
In the next row: P5(7, 9, 11, 13), cast on 7(9, 11, 13, 15) stitches, p26(36, 46, 56, 66), cast on 7(9, 11, 13, 15) stitches, purl to end of row.
Work in Stockinette Stitch until back measures 5(9, 13, 17, 21) inches from leash hole and bind off loosely.

### Optional sleeves
Using DPNs, pick up and knit 8(10, 12, 14, 16) stitches along each edge of the sleeve opening—16(20, 24, 28, 32) stitches. (Make sure to pick up the stitches on the edges from the body and not the steek stitches.)

Work in k2, p2 rib for 1(1.5, 2, 3, 4) inches. Bind off loosely.

Working from the wrong side of the sweater, cut the steeks down the center. Fold them back and, with a yarn needle and waste yarn, tack the cut edges down inside the body of the sweater, going through the first complete stitch on the edge of the steek and the purl bumps on the inside of the sweater.

Use Mattress Stitch to seam up the stomach and chest of the sweater. Remember that the turtleneck will be folded over and should be seamed from the right side so that the seam is hidden when it's worn.

Wash by hand in cold water and block gently as Noro Kureyon will felt when machine washed.

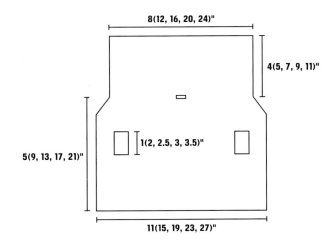

8(12, 16, 20, 24)"
4(5, 7, 9, 11)"
1(2, 2.5, 3, 3.5)"
5(9, 13, 17, 21)"
11(15, 19, 23, 27)"

# Nightwalker Sport Coat

*Designed by Staceyjoy Elkin, Pattern by Amy Swenson*

If you ever doubted it, this big boy jacket makes it clear: dog coats are not just for poodles anymore. This handsome red sport coat is just the thing to knit for L and XL dogs. Reflective racing stripes down each side complete the sporty look, and protect both dog and owner should they decide to take a night walk.

## MATERIALS:

* Debbie Bliss Merino Aran (100% merino wool, 86 yds per 50g ball); Color: 700 Red; 6(7, 9, 10, 13) balls

* US 8/5 mm needles
  (or size needed to match gauge)

* Stitch markers
* Cable needle

* 1-inch wide reflective tape—40(48, 56, 60, 64) inches
* Thread to match reflective tape

## GAUGE

18 stitches/24 rows = 4 inches in Stockinette Stitch

## SIZE

**Dog's chest measurement:** 22(26, 30, 34, 38) inches
**Sweater length:** 20(24, 28, 30, 32) inches

## SWEATER

### Back

Cast on 66(70, 78, 86, 98) stitches.
Row 1: P2, [k2, p2] 2(2, 3, 3, 4) times, work Row 1 of Chart A, [p2, k2] 4(5, 5, 7, 8) times, p2, work Row 1 of Chart A, [p2, k2] 2(2, 3, 3, 4) times, p2.

Row 2: K2, [p2, k2] 2(2, 3, 3, 4) times, work Row 2 of Chart A, [k2, p2] 4(5, 5, 7, 8) times, k2, work Row 2 of Chart A, [k2, p2] 2(2, 3, 3, 4) times, k2.

## Chart A

(Chart A grid with rows numbered 4, 3, 2, 1)

☐ K (RS)

— P (RS)

⬛ Slip next 2 stitches to cable needle and hold to Back of work. K2, k2 from cable needle.

⬛ Slip next 2 stitches to cable needle and hold to Front of work. K2, k2 from cable needle.

Continue in pattern as set until 4 rows of Chart A have been worked 6(6, 6, 7, 7) times.

On next right side row, increase as follows:
P2 [k1, m1, k1, p1, m1, p1] 2(2, 3, 3, 4) times, work Row 1 of Chart A, [p1, m1, p1, k1, m1, k1] 4(5, 5, 7, 8) times, p1, m1, p1, work Row 1 of Chart A, [p1, m1, p1, k1, m1, k1] 2(2, 3, 3, 4) times, p2 83(89, 101, 113, 131) stitches.

K2[p3, k3] 2(2, 3, 3, 4) times, work next row of Chart A, [k3, p3] 4(5, 5, 7, 8) times, k3, work next row of Chart A, [k3, p3] 2(2, 3, 3, 4) times, k2.

Beginning with next row, work in Broken Rib as follows:
Row 1: P2, 12(12, 18, 18, 24), work next row of Chart A, k27(33, 33, 45, 51), work next row of Chart A, 12(12, 18, 18, 24), p2.

Row 2: K2[p3, k3] 2(2, 3, 3, 4) times, work next Row of Chart A, [k3, p3] 4(5, 5, 7, 8) times, k3, work next row of Chart A, [k3, p3] 2(2, 3, 3, 4) times, k2.

Continue in pattern as set until back panel measures 17.5(21.5, 25, 27, 29) inches from cast on edge, or to 3 inches less than desired length, ending with a WS row.

On next RS row, decrease as follows:
P2 [k2tog, k1, p2tog, p1] 2(2, 3, 3, 4) times, work next row of Chart A, [p2tog, p1, k2tog, k1] 4(5, 5, 7, 8) times, p2tog, p1, work next row of Chart A, [p2tog, p1, k2tog, k1] 2(2, 3, 3, 4) times, p2. 66(70, 78, 86, 98) stitches.

K2, [p2, k2] 2(2, 3, 3, 4) times, work next row of Chart A, [k2, p2] 4(5, 5, 7, 8) times, k2, work next row of Chart A, [k2, p2] 2(2, 3, 3, 4) times, k2.

Continue in Rib as set, working stitches as they appear until bottom Rib is 3-inches long or as desired. Bind off all stitches.

## Front

Cast on 7 stitches.

Row 1: P2, k3, p2.
Row 2: K2, p3, k2.
Row 3: P2, m1 purlwise, k3, m1 purlwise, p2—9 stitches.
Row 4: K3, p3, k3.
Row 5: P3, m1 knitwise, k3, m1 knitwise, p3—11 stitches.
Row 6: K3, p5, k3.
Row 7: P3, K1, m1 knitwise, k3, m1 knitwise, k1, p3—13 stitches.

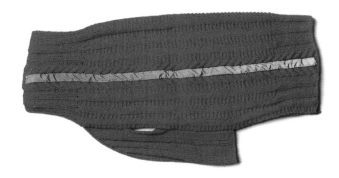

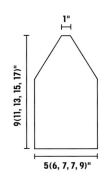

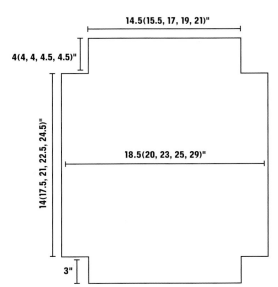

Row 8: K3, p7, k3.
Row 9: P3, k2, m1 purlwise, k3, m1 purlwise, k2, p3—15 stitches.
Row 10: K3, p2, k1, p3, k1, p2, k3.
Row 11: P3, k2, p1, m1 purlwise, k3, m1 purlwise, p1, k2, p3—17 stitches.
Row 12: K3, p2, k2, p3, k2, p2, k3.

Continue working increases either side of center k3, working new stitches into k2, p2 rib as established until there are 17(27, 33, 33, 41) stitches.

Continue even in pattern as set until front panel measures 9(11, 13, 15, 17) inches from cast on edge, or until length desired. Bind off all stitches.

### FINISHING

Cut reflective tape into two even lengths. Attach one piece to each six-stitch-wide Reverse Stockinette Stitch portion of the back panel (between pairs of cables) with sewing needle and thread.

Place the point of the front at the V just below the ribbed collar you have seamed. Seam about an inch on either side of the point. A fitting on your dog now will help you determine the size and position of the armholes. Seam Front to Back on either side from the cast on edge of the Front to just behind the forelegs.

# Houndstooth Hunting Jacket

*By Kristi Porter*

Here is a comfortable, functional jacket to keep your dog warm on even the most chilly days. The dashing Houndstooth Pattern (an obvious choice for canines!) features bright contrasting colors sewn to two insulating layers of polar fleece. Whether he's chasing wild game or tennis balls, this easy-on, easy-off jacket will keep your favorite hunter cozy.

The Houndstooth Pattern looks impressive, but it is quite simple to knit. You will be working with only one color at a time. Really, there is little more to it than knitting stripes, alternating colors every two rows. The color patterning is achieved by slipping stitches every right side row to create the houndstooth check.

## MATERIALS

* [MC] Cascade 220 (100% superwash wool; 220 yds per 100g skein); Color: 822; 1(1, 1, 1 1) skein
* [CC] Cascade 220 Tweed (100% wool; 220 yds per 100g skein); Color: 7610; 1(1, 1, 1, 1) skein
* 1 set US 8/5 mm needles (or size needed to match gauge)
* 0.75(1, 1, 1, 1.25) yd fleece fabric in coordinating color
* Sewing thread to match fabric
* 3 heavy duty sew-on snaps
* 3 buttons (just for show!)

## GAUGE

18 stitches/26 rows = 4 inches in Houndstooth Pattern

## SIZE

**Dog's chest measurement:** 18(22, 26, 30, 34) inches
**Sweater width:** 12(14.5, 17, 20, 22.5)
**Sweater body length:** 11(14, 16, 18, 20)

(Length should be two inches shorter than your dog's measurement from collar to base of tail. Add or subtract rows where advised in the pattern for a custom fit.)

## TECHNIQUES

### Houndstooth Pattern

(worked over a multiple of 3 stitches)

Row 1 (right side): With MC, k1, *sl 1 stitch purlwise with yib, k2, repeat from * to last 2 stitches, sl 1, k1.
Row 2: With MC, purl.
Row 3: With CC, *sl 1 stitch purlwise with yarn in back, k2, repeat from * to end of row.
Row 4: With CC, purl.

## JACKET

### Body

With MC, cast on 36(42, 45, 54, 60) stitches. On the next row, begin working Row 1 of Houndstooth Pattern. Increase 1 stitch at each end on every wrong side (purl) row 9(12, 15, 18, 21) times to 54(66, 75, 90, 102) stitches.

Continue in Houndstooth Pattern until piece measures 10(13, 15, 17, 19) inches or desired length, ending with a WS row.

Note: When working increases or decreases, make sure that the slipped stitches line up with slipped stitches of the same color on previous rows. To do this, always begin by knitting the first stitch in the working color for that row. Knit one or two more stitches before slipping for the first time in order to line up the slipped stitches with previous same-color rows.

### Neck Shaping

Next row: Work in Houndstooth Pattern across first 17(20, 23, 26, 29) stitches, bind off center 20(26, 29, 38, 44) stitches, continue in Houndstooth Pattern to end of row.

Continue working each side of neck separately in Houndstooth Pattern, decreasing 1 stitch at neck edge every wrong side (purl) row, 4 times until 13(16, 19, 22, 25) stitches remain on each side. Work even until shoulder pieces measure 3(3.75, 4, 5, 5.75) inches from first neck decrease.
Bind off all stitches.

## FINISHING

Using MC and crochet hook, work single crochet around all edges of finished piece. Block knitted piece and weave in ends on wrong side of work.

Lay blocked piece out on two layers of polar fleece and pin the three layers together. Cut two layers of polar fleece lining 2 inches larger than finished knitted piece with 3 inches of fleece beyond neck ends as shown in sketch opposite.

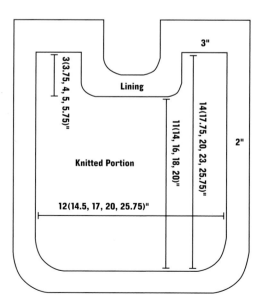

Do not sew the two openings at the neck! Trim all seams to ¼ inch, and snip into the curves of the seam allowance to make the piece lie smooth when turned right side out.

Turn piece right side out carefully through the neck edge opening and flatten seams with your fingers. Do not iron polar fleece!

Turn each side of the neck under approximately 1 inch. Seam closed by hand or machine.

Try the jacket on your dog and mark the best placement for closure on the belly band. Attach two snaps to the neck opening and one snap to the belly band. If desired, sew decorative buttons on the public side to cover the snaps.

Cut one strip of polar fleece measuring approximately 9 inches wide and 11 (12, 14, 15, 16) inches long for belly band.

Fold belly band in half and sew together along 3 remaining sides. Cut in two pieces with one piece approximately twice as long as the other. Trim seams to 0.25 inch and trim corner. Turn pieces right side out.

Try one layer of polar fleece on your dog and mark appropriate placement for belly band behind forelegs. Pin belly-band pieces to one layer of lining, allow for 4 inches of overlap of the two belly-band pieces. Baste in place with the bands facing in to the center of lining. Trim excess off ends of bands. Set aside.

With a needle and thread or sewing machine, carefully sew the knitted jacket to the other layer of the lining at the edge of the knitted piece.

Put the two lining layers together with right sides facing and bands and knitted layer inside the sandwich. Pin layers carefully. Sew a seam, by hand or machine, along the U of the neckline. Sew the jacket along the outside edges.

**Belly Band**
**showing cut line and snap placement**

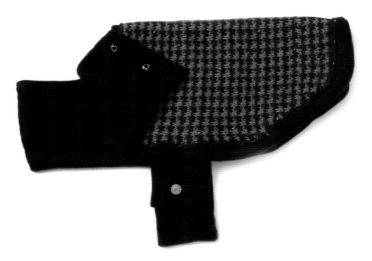

# Rain-Resistant Coat and Hoodie

*Designed by Staceyjoy Elkin, Pattern by Amy Swenson*

The yarn used in this sporty raincoat and hood has been treated with Teflon to not only keep your dog warm, but dry as well. The neck and belly feature ribbed panels to provide a better fit. You can easily alter the length of the sweater or the width by adding or subtracting repeats of the ribbing pattern as desired for a snuggly fit.

## MATERIALS

* Dale of Norway Hauk (100% new wool treated with Teflon, 108 yds per 50g ball):
  [MC] Color: 5545 Pansy Blue; 5(6, 7, 8) balls
  [CC] Color: 3418 Burnt Orange; 1(2, 2, 3) balls

* 1 set US 5/3.75 mm needles
* 1 12-inch long US 5/3.75 mm circular needle (or size needed to match gauge)
* Size G/4 mm crochet hook

* Stitch markers
* Cable needle

## GAUGE

24 stitches/28 rows to 4 inches in Stockinette Stitch

## SIZE

**Sweater**
**Dog's chest measurement:** 18(22, 26, 30) inches
**Sweater length:** 16.5(19, 24, 29) inches

**Hood**
**Finished width:** 13.5(16, 19, 22)
**Finished length:** 10(12, 15, 17)

## RAINCOAT

### Back

The Back is knit flat. Cast on 84(100, 116, 132) stitches with MC.

Row 1: K1 (selvage stitch), follow Chart for Raincoat, Section A 3(4, 5, 6) times, Section B 1 time, Section C 3(4, 5, 6) times, k1 (selvage stitch).

Continue as set for Rows 1-16, always knitting the first and last stitch of every row to create the selvage edge.

Continue knitting from the Chart for Rows 17–32, maintaining pattern as set across Chart for Raincoat. After Row 32, repeat from Rows 17–32 5(6, 8,10) times more or to length desired.

### Bottom Ribbing

K1 (selvage stitch), work Row 33 of Section A 3(4, 5, 6) times, Section B, Section C 3(4, 5, 6) times, k1 (selvage stitch). Continue in rib as set in Row 33 for 5 more rows. Bind off all stitches in rib.

# Chart for Raincoat

**Section C**        **Section B**        **Section A**

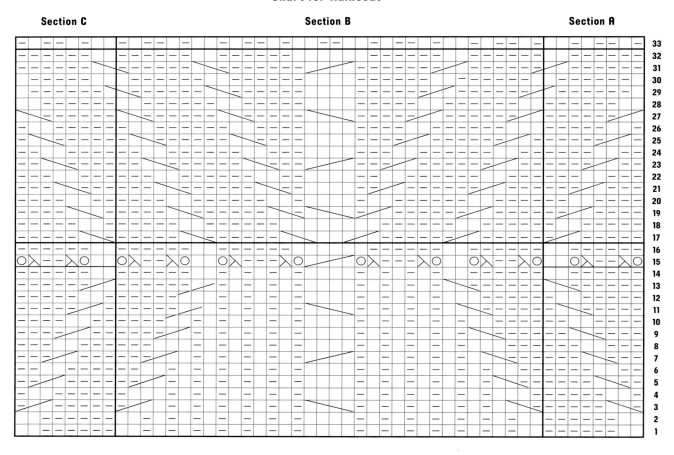

K on RS, p on WS

p on RS, k on WS

3st RC – Slip next stitch to cable needle and hold to Back of work. K2, p1 from cable needle.

Slip next 2 stitches to cable needle and hold to Front of work. P1, k2 from cable needle.

4st RC – Slip next 2 stitches to cable needle and hold to Back of work. K2, k2 from cable needle.

4st LC – Slip next 2 stitches to cable needle and hold to Front of work. K2, k2 from cable needle.

YO

p2tog

## Front

Cast on 3 stitches with MC.

Row 1: K1, place marker, k1, place marker, k1.

Row 2: P3.

Row 3: K1, m1, k1, m1, k1 (5 stitches).

Row 4: K2, p1, k2.

Row 5: K1, p1, m1, k1, m1, p1, k1 (7 stitches).

Row 6: K2, p3, k2.

Row 7: K1, p1, k1, m1, k1, m1, k1, p1, k1 (9 stitches).

Continue increasing this way, working increases in k1, p1 rib until there are 13(21, 29, 37) stitches. Continue in rib as established, without further shaping, until front panel measures 9(10, 12, 15) inches from cast on edge. Bind off in rib.

## Tie

With MC and crochet hook, chain 80(90, 120, 140) or until length desired.

## FINISHING

Fold Back in half, lengthwise, and sew neck seam together to 1 inch past eyelet row. Place the point of the front at the V just below the ribbed collar you have seamed. Seam about an inch on either side of the point. A fitting on your dog now will help you determine the size and position of the armholes. Seam Front to Back on either side from the cast on edge of the Front to just behind the forelegs. Thread tie through eyelets and tie at top with bow to secure.

## HOOD

With CC and circular needle, cast on 80(96, 112, 128) stitches and join to begin working in the round, being careful not to twist. Work Chart for Hood in the round for rounds 1-10.

Round 11: [3stLC, k1, p4] around.
Round 12: [P1, k3, p4] around.

## Chart for Hood

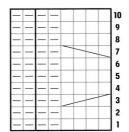

Round 13: [P1, 3stLC, p4] around.
Round 14: [P2, k2, p4] around.
Round 15: [P2, 2stLC, p3] around.
Round 16: [P3, k2, p3] around.
Round 17: [P3, 2stLC, p2] around.
Round 18: [P4, k2, p2] around.
Round 19: [P4, 2stLC, p1] around.
Round 20: [P5, k2, p1] around.
Round 21: [P5, 2stLC] around.
Round 22: [P6, k2] around.

Repeat Rounds 1-22 until piece measures 10(12, 15, 17) inches from cast on edge. Bind off all stitches.

# Raglan Monogrammed Sweater

*Designed by Staceyjoy Elkin, Pattern by Kate Watson*

Your dog will look collegiate in this classic raglan pullover, a sporty option for small and large dogs. The tapered design makes it perfect for athletic activity of all kinds, whether your pup likes to catch Frisbees or just play chase. The monogrammed letter lets everyone know who's champ.

## MATERIALS

* Karabella Aurora 8 (100% merino wool; 98 yds per 50g skein):
    [MC] 01 Mélange; 2(2, 4, 5, 7) skeins
    [CC1] 07 Bright Red; 1(1, 2, 2, 2) skeins
    [CC2] 08 Orange; 1 skein
* 1 set US 8/5 mm needles
    (or size needed to match gauge)
* 1 G/4 mm crochet hook

## GAUGE

17 stitches/20 rows = 4 inches in Stockinette Stitch

## SIZE

**Dog's chest measurement:** 10(14, 18, 22, 26) inches
**Finished length:** 13(17, 21, 25, 29) inches, or to fit

## SWEATER

### Back

The Back is knit from neck to tail.

With MC, cast on 22(30, 38, 46, 54) stitches.

*Work in k1, p1 rib for 1 inch. Change to CC2 and work in rib for 2 rows. Change to MC and continue in rib for 0.5(1, 1.5, 2, 2.5) inches. Change to CC2 and work in rib for 2 rows. Return to MC and continue in rib until piece measures 2.5(3, 3.5, 4, 4.5) inches from beginning, ending with a RS row.
P1 row.*

Working in Stockinette Stitch, increase 1 stitch at each edge of next row and every following alternate row 7(9, 12, 14, 17) times 38(50, 64, 76, 90) stitches.

Work even in Stockinette Stitch until piece measures 6(10, 14, 18, 22) inches from beginning, or to three inches less than desired length, ending with a WS row. Work in k1, p1 rib for 4 rows. **Change to CC2 and work in rib for 2 rows. Change to MC and work in rib for 4 rows.** Rep from ** to ** 1 time more. Bind off all stitches.

### Front

The Front is knit from neck to belly.

With MC, cast on 12(18, 20, 26, 28) stitches. Work as for Back from * to *. Work even in Stockinette Stitch until piece measures 3(6, 9, 12, 15) inches from beginning, adjusting length by same amount as Back, if necessary, ending with a WS row.
Work in k1, p1 rib for 3 inches. Bind off all stiches.

### Optional Sleeves (make 2)

With CC1, cast on 22(28, 36, 42, 50) stitches. Work in k1, p1 rib for 3 rows. Change to CC2 and work in rib for 2 rows. Change to CC1 and continue in rib until piece measures 1.5(1.5, 2, 2, 2) inches from beginning, ending with RS facing. Work 2(2, 4, 6, 8) rows even in Stockinette Stitch.
Working in Stockinette Stitch, decrease 1 stitch at each edge of next and every following alternate row 7(9, 12, 14, 17) times to 4(6, 8, 10, 12) stitches. Work 1 row even. Bind off.

### FINISHING

Beginning at neck, and using mattress stitch, sew Front to Back to beginning of back raglan shaping. Sew raglan sleeve caps to Front and Back pieces, matching raglan shaping on Back to raglan shaping on sleeve, and sewing remaining raglan edge of sleeve along straight edge of Front. Sew straight edges of sleeves together. Finish sewing Back to Front.

## MONOGRAMMING BASICS

Sure, your hand-knit sweater stands out from the crowd and is unlikely to be confused with the other mascot's sweater (unless you're outfitting a whole litter of pups!), but why not add a monogram to this go-team-go sweater? You can use your dog's initial, your own, or let him root for the alma mater.

If you don't have a knitting guide with an alphabet handy, here's how to do it from scratch: Take a sheet of graph paper and mark out a rectangle about 15 squares tall and 7- to 10-squares wide. Remember that knitting stitches are wider than they are tall, so you'll want your letter to look extra tall on paper. (If you have knitter's graph paper, you won't have to worry!) Use fonts in books, magazines or the computer to inspire you and sketch away.

If you are more graphics savvy, type your letter in a small font in a graphic design program, scale the height by 120% and blow it up so you can see the pixels. Voila! Instant knitting chart of your favorite font!

Once you've got your chart, use a crocheted slip stitch, or a tapestry needle and duplicate stitch (also called Swiss darning), or even a cross stitch to apply your design in one of your contrasting colors.

You don't have to limit yourself to initials, of course: Consider some other icon that symbolizes your dog or your team.

If desired, use crochet hook to slip stitch chosen letter motif, centered on Back at top of bottom ribbing, in both CC1 and CC2. Alternatively, use tapestry needle and duplicate stitch (or Swiss darning) to apply motif in contrasting colors.
Weave in all ends.
Block if desired.

# Haute Coats

Anyone who has ever owned a dog knows they can be uncouth. They snatch whatever scraps fall from the table, revel in scents that make us blush, and chase anything that will run from them. But even the most rough-and-tumble dog loves to be praised. So dress her up in a Faux Fur Glamour Coat, Sequined Princess Sweater, or other haute coat and tell her how pretty she looks. If you shower her with compliments, maybe she'll be distracted from that slice of cake she's been eyeing.

* **Popcorn Matinee Sweater**
* **Sequined Princess Sweater**
* **Woodland Sweater**
* **Faux Fur Glamour Coat**
* **Fancy Lacy Capelet**

# Popcorn Matinee Sweater

*Designed by Staceyjoy Elkin, Pattern by Heather Brack*

**This whimsical sweater, decorated with knitted bobbles, will look as cute as a button on your pooch. While Fifi might not be welcome at the theater, you'll both be happy curled up on a chilly day watching *Lassie Come Home*.**

## MATERIALS

* [MC] Cascade 220 (100% wool, 220 yds per 100g skein); Color: 9434; 1(1, 2, 3, 3) skeins
* [CC] Noro Kureyon (100% wool, 110 yds per 50g skein); Color: 52; 1(1, 2, 2, 2) skeins

* 1 set US 7/4.5 mm needles (or size to match gauge)

* Stitch markers
* Stitch holders

## GAUGE

18 stitches/28 rows = 4 inches in Stockinette Stitch

## SIZES

**Dog's chest measurement:** 10(14, 18, 22, 26) inches
**Finished length:** 8(13, 16, 20, 24) inches

The sweater is designed to cover your dog's back all the way to her tail. Feel free to customize this length if your dog has a longer or shorter back measurement, but make sure to buy extra yarn if you plan on lengthening it.

## TECHNIQUES

### Bobble Stitch

Using CC, knit 5 times into one stitch: into the front, then the back, front, back, front of the stitch.
Turn work and p5.
Turn work and k5.
Turn work and p5.
Turn work and k5tog tbl.
Switch back to MC.

## SWEATER

### Neck

Using MC, cast on 38(54, 74, 90, 110) stitches.
Work in k2, p2 rib for 4(5, 7, 9, 11) inches.

### Body

Row 1: Knit.

Row 2 and following even rows: Purl.

Row 3: K1, k1fb, place marker, k1, k across to last 3 stitches, place marker, k1fb, k2.

Row 5: K1, make bobble, k1fb, slip marker. *Make bobble, k3. Repeat from * to second marker, slip marker, k1fb, make bobble, k2.

Row 7: K3, k1fb, slip marker, k3, k to second marker, slip marker, k1fb, k to end.

Row 9: K2, make bobble, k1, k1fb, slip marker. *K1, make bobble, k2. Repeat from * to second marker, slip marker, k1fb, k1, make bobble, k to end.

Row 11: K5, k1fb, slip marker, k to second marker, slip marker, k1fb, k to end.

Row 13: K3, make bobble, k2, k1fb, slip marker. *K2, make bobble, k1. Repeat from * to marker, slip marker, k1fb, k2, make bobble, k to end.

Row 15: K7, k1fb, slip marker, k across to marker, slip marker, k1fb, k to end—52(68, 88, 104, 124) stitches on needles.

Row 17: K4, make bobble, k to marker, slip marker. *K3, make bobble. Repeat from * to second marker, slip marker, k4, make bobble, k4.

Row 19: Knit all stitches.

Row 21: K to marker, work bobble pattern starting at Row 3 of Chart A until second marker, k to end.

Continue working Stomach (outside of markers) in Stockinette Stitch and Back (between markers) according to Chart A for 1(1.5, 2, 3, 3.5) inches, ending on a knit row with bobbles. Purl 1 row.

### Armholes

K 5(7, 9, 11, 13) stitches, bind off 5(7, 9, 11, 13), k 30(40, 50, 60, 70) stitches, bind off 5(7, 9, 11, 13), k to end.

Slip first 5(7, 9, 11, 13) stitches and center 32(40, 52, 60, 72) to stitch holders.

Continue to work remaining 5(7, 9, 11, 13) stitches in Stockinette Stitch for 1(2, 2.5, 3, 3.5) inches, ending with a purl row. Slip these stitches to stitch holder and break yarn.

Transfer 32(40, 52, 60, 72) Back Stitches from stitch holder to needles and continue to work according to Chart A for 1.5(2, 2.5, 3, 3.5) inches, ending with a purl row. Break yarn and transfer to stitch holder.

**Chart A**      **Chart B**

Transfer 5(7, 9, 11, 13) from remaining stitch holder to needles and work in Stockinette Stitch for 1(2, 2.5, 3, 3.5) inches, ending with a purl row.

Finish the armholes in the next row:
Knit 5(7, 9, 11, 13) stitches, cast on 5(7, 9, 11, 13), knit 32(40, 52, 60, 72) Back stitches from stitch holder, cast on 5(7, 9, 11, 13), knit remaining 5(7, 9, 11, 13) stitches from remaining stitch holder. 52(68, 88, 104, 124) stitches on needles.

Work in k2, p2 ribbing until Back measures 4(8, 12, 16, 20) inches from base of neck (beginning of stomach shaping).

Bind off 5(7, 9, 11, 13) stitches in pattern, work 42(54, 70, 82, 98) stitches in pattern, bind off to end of row in pattern. Break yarn.

Reattach yarn and continue to work remaining stitches in k2, p2 ribbing until back measures 6(11, 14, 18, 22) inches from base of neck, ending with a WS row.

Next row: Work 4 stitch repeat of Row 1 of Chart B to last 2 stitches. K2. Continue in pattern as set until all rows of Chart B have been worked.

Work in k2, p2 rib for 4 rows. Bind off all stitches loosely in pattern.

## FINISHING

Use Mattress Stitch to sew the stomach and chest seams of the sweater. Remember that the turtleneck will be folded over and should be seamed from the right side so that the seam is hidden when it's worn. Weave in ends.

Wash by hand in cold water and block gently.

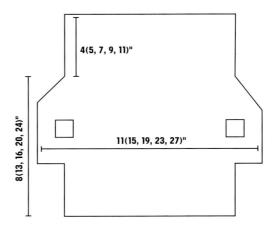

4(5, 7, 9, 11)"

8(13, 16, 20, 24)"

11(15, 19, 23, 27)"

# Sequined Princess Sweater

*By Kristi Porter*

What do you knit for the dog you treat like royalty? A princess sweater of course! This sparkly ruffled little number is suitable for the most special occasions...whether your pup's eating kibble from a crystal goblet or attending a New Year's Eve fête. Your precious pooch is a boy? He'll look princely in the golden version of this sweater.

A couple of tips for happy knitting: For the neck ruffle on larger sweaters, it's helpful to work with two circular needles in the round as the stitch count is quadrupled. Also, to prevent irksome tangles, put the sequined Lazer FX in a baggie that's zipped almost all the way closed; the working thread exits smoothly though the small opening.

## MATERIALS

**For variegated silver princess sweater:**

* [MC] Berroco Quest (100% nylon; 82 yds per 50g skein); Color: 9934 (variegated silver); 1(3, 4, 6, 8) skeins
* [CC] Berroco Lazer FX (100% polyester; 70 yds per 10g skein); Color 6005 (silver); 1(3, 5, 7, 9) skeins

**For golden prince sweater:**

* [MC] Berroco Quest (100% nylon; 82 yds per 50g skein); Color 9812 (gold); 1 (3, 4, 6, 8) skeins
* [CC] Berroco Lazer FX (100% polyester; 70 yds per 10g skein); Color 6003 (gold); 1 (3, 5, 7, 9) skeins
* 1 set US 8/5 mm needles
* 1 set US 6/4 mm needles
* 1 set US 6/4 mm DPNs (or with a second circular to knit in the round on two circular needles)

(or sizes needed to match gauge)

## GAUGE

16 stitches/20 rows = 4 inches
in Stockinette Stitch on larger needles

20 stitches/28 rows = 4 inches
in k1, p1 rib on smaller needles

## SIZE

**Dog's chest measurement:** 10(14, 18, 22, 26) inches
**Finished length:** 8(12, 16, 21, 23) inches

(Length should be 2 inches shorter than dog's measurement from collar to base of tail.)

### Back

The back is knit from neck to tail.

With MC, cast on 28(44, 60, 76, 80) stitches on larger needles. Attach CC and work with both yarns held together, back and forth in Stockinette Stitch until piece measures 5.25(9, 12, 16, 17) inches (or your dog's length from collar to base of tail minus 4(5, 6, 7, 8) inches).

Decrease 1 stitch at each side every right side row, until piece measures 7(11, 15, 20, 22) inches. Drop CC and bind off remaining 20(34, 46, 56, 56) stitches with MC only.

## Front

The front is knitted from the belly up to the neck.

With MC only and smaller needles, cast on 15(23, 27, 35, 43) stitches. Attach CC and, with both yarns held together, work in k1, p1 rib for 2.5(4.5, 7.5, 9, 9) inches. (If you have made Back longer or shorter for a custom fit, add or subtract the same number of inches here!)

Decrease 1 stitch at each side every 3rd row 4(8, 10, 14, 18) times. Work 2 more rows on remaining 7 stitches. Piece should measure 4.25(8, 12.25, 15.75, 16.75) inches. Drop CC and bind off all stitches in rib with MC only.

Tack smaller end of Front to larger end of Back at either side. Leave foreleg holes (decrease portion of Front) open. Seam together Front and Back along flat edges. Ruffle will be picked up around neck and along the shaped portion of the Back.

## Ruffle

The ruffle, worked back and forth along the rump, will quadruple the number of stitches on the needle.

Working on the right side with MC only and smaller needles, pick up and knit 34(54, 74, 94, 104) along the back end of the sweater, from the points where Back and Front are attached on each side. Knit 1 row. On the next row, knit into the front and back of each stitch. Knit 1 row.

Next row: [K1, YO] across. Knit 1 row. Bind off all stitches.

## Neck Ruffle

With MC only, using DPNs or 2 circular needles of smaller gauge to work in the round, pick up and knit 32(48, 64, 80, 84) stitches around neck edge on the right side of the sweater. Knit 1 round. Next round: Knit into the front and back of each stitch. Purl 1 round. Next round: [K1, YO] around. Purl 1 round. Bind off all stitches.

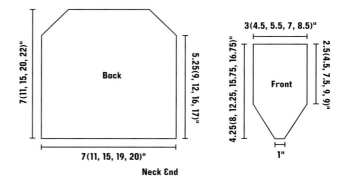

**Back** — 7(11, 15, 20, 22)" · 5.25(9, 12, 16, 17)" · 7(11, 15, 19, 20)" · Neck End

**Front** — 3(4.5, 5.5, 7, 8.5)" · 2.5(4.5, 7.5, 9, 9)" · 4.25(8, 12.25, 15.75, 16.75)" · 1"

## FINISHING

Weave in all ends. If necessary, carefully cut the sequins from the binding thread to make weaving ends in easier. After trying the sweater on your dog, you may wish to sew the foreleg holes smaller for a custom fit. With a crochet hook and MC only, work a round of single crochet around leg openings.

# Woodland Sweater

*Designed by Staceyjoy Elkin, Pattern by Amy Swenson*

Every dog enjoys a tromp through the woods and this vine-covered wood-grain-patterned coat reflects his desire to get back to nature. The fit on this coat, with a buttoned belly strap, is easy and comfortable and will fit dogs of all shapes and sizes. You can alter the length by adding or subtracting repeats of the chart before beginning the neck shaping.

## MATERIALS

* Koigu Kersti (100% merino wool; 114 yds per 50 g skein):

    [MC] Color: K-0000 White; 1(2, 3, 5) skeins
    [CC1] Color: K-1300 Brown; 1(1, 2, 5) skeins
    [CC2] Color: K-514 Green mix; 1(1, 1, 1) skein

Because Koigu yarns are hand-dyed in individual lots of twenty, you may not be able to exactly replicate the color mix as shown for the green ivy. Koigu's Kersti is distributed with several green variations, all of which would work nicely for the vine detailing.

* 1 set US 6/4 mm needles
* 1 12-inch US 6/4 mm circular needle or double pointed needles for neck
* 1 30-inch US 6/4 mm circular needle for edging
* 1 set US 6/4 DPNs

* Stitch markers
* Cable needle
* Stitch holder
* 1 button

## GAUGE

22 stitches/28 rows = 4 inches in Stockinette Stitch

## SIZE

**Dog's chest measurement:** 14(18, 26, 34) inches
**Finished sweater length:** 11(15, 19, 28) inches
**Neck opening:** 10(13, 17, 20) inches

## SWEATER

### Body

With MC and straight needles, cast on 48(72, 96, 120) stitches. Purl 1 row (WS). Work Chart A in Stockinette Stitch, beginning with a RS row. Continue to work following chart, working Rows 1-32 2(3, 4, 6) times. Work Rows 1-6 1 more time.

### Neck shaping

While continuing to work following Chart A, shape the neck as follows:

Work 18(27, 36, 45) stitches. Place these stitches on a holder. Bind off next 12(18, 24, 30) stitches, work remaining stitches.

Place first 18(27, 36, 45) stitches on a holder and set aside.

Decrease 1 stitch at neck edge on every RS row 2(3, 5, 7) times. 16(24, 31, 38) stitches remain.
Continue without shaping for an additional 24(32, 36, 40) rows.
Bind off all stitches.

Place held stitches on needles and work to match, reversing shaping.

**Chart A**

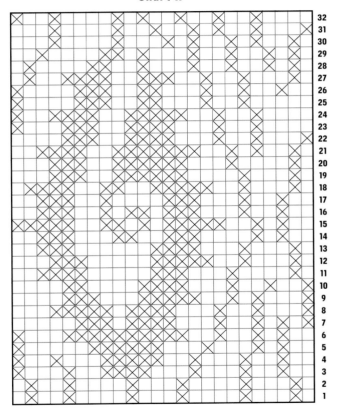

⊠ Brown 1300　　☐ White 0000

## Chart B

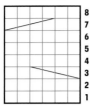

| | | | | | | |
|---|---|---|---|---|---|---|
8
7
6
5
4
3
2
1

| | |
|---|---|
| ![RC symbol] | **4st RC – Slip next 2 stitches to cable needle and hold to Back of work. K2, k2 from cable needle.** |
| ![LC symbol] | **4st LC – Slip next 2 stitches to cable needle and hold to Front of work. K2, k2 from cable needle.** |

### Belly Strap

With MC and straight needles, cast on 12(12, 16, 16) stitches.

K3(3, 5, 5), work Chart B over 6 stitches, k3(3, 5, 5).

Continue as set, working edge stitches in Garter Stitch and center stitches following Chart B, until strap is 4(4, 9, 13) inches long or as desired.

On next RS row, k3(3, 5, 5), bind off next 6 stitches, k3(3, 5, 5).

Turn work, K3(3, 5, 5), cast on 6 stitches with backward loop method, k3(3, 5, 5).

Knit 4 additional rows.

Bind off all stitches.

### FINISHING

Sew top ends of sweater together to form front seam.

### Edging

With longer circular needles and MC, pick up and knit 48(72, 96, 120) stitches along bottom edge, place marker, 78(114, 150, 210) stitches along side to front seam, and 78(114, 150, 210) stitches along remaining side.

Place marker, join to begin working in the round.

[P 6, work Chart B over 6 stitches] around, increasing 1 stitch purlwise at each side of markers, incorporating increased stitches into pattern as set. (4 stitches increased each round.)

Repeat for 8 rounds.

Switch to CC1 and work one round as follows:

[P6, k6] around without increasing.

Switch to MC and purl 1 round.

Bind off all stitches.

## Neck

With shorter circular needle and MC, pick up and knit 60(84, 108, 120) stitches around neck. Place marker, join, and continue in rounds.

[P6, work chart B over 6 stitches] around.
Repeat for 18 rounds.
Switch to CC1 and work one round as follows:
[P6, K6] around.
Switch to MC and p1 round.
Bind off all stitches.

Sew end of belly strap to edging approximately halfway from neck to tail. Line up with other side of coat to position button. Sew button in place.

## Leaves

Make 5(7, 9, 11) leaves.
With CC2, cast on 3 stitches.
K1, place marker, k1, place marker, k1.
Continue in Garter Stitch, increasing as follows every other row:
Knit to marker, m1, slip marker, k1, slip marker, m1, knit to end.

Continue as set until there are 29 stitches. Knitting (and increasing) additional rows will make a larger leaf. Bind off all stitches.

## Vine

With DPNs and CC2, cast on 4 stitches.
Make icord as follows **k4, do not turn. Slide stitches to right end of needle.**

Repeat from ** to ** until Vine is 15(20, 25, 35) inches long or as desired. Cut yarn and pull through stitches to bind off. (You can always prune later by cutting off part of the vine and securing the loose end.)

Sew vine to coat, attaching leaves as desired using photograph as a guide.

Weave in all ends. Block if desired.

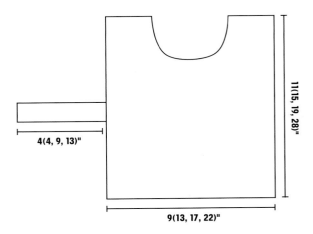

4(4, 9, 13)"

11(15, 19, 28)"

9(13, 17, 22)"

# Faux Fur Glamour Coat

*By Amy Swenson*

Dogs with short fur will appreciate this faux fur coat during the chillier months. The yarn is held doubled to make the coat extra plush and oh so glamorous. Take care when choosing a size: this yarn makes an extremely stretchy fabric! To ensure a good fit, finished sizes are given in an already stretched state. Use these measurements to determine the right size for your dog, rather than by knitting a swatch to check the gauge. The sweater will stretch more in width than length, so if you wish to make the sweater longer, keep this in mind. If the coat is too stretchy around the neck, you can crochet a single row of stitches with the same yarn for a closer fit.

## MATERIALS

* OnLine Smash Print (100% acrylic; 100 yds per 50g skein); Color: 105; 2(2, 2, 3) balls (Yarn is held doubled throughout.)

* 1 set US 10/6 mm needles (or size needed to match gauge)

## GAUGE

9 stitches/12 rows = 4 inches in Garter Stitch with yarn held doubled

## SIZE

**Sweater chest measurement (stretched):**
12(16, 20, 24) inches
**Neck:** 8(10, 12, 14) inches
**Sweater length:** 10(12, 14, 16) inches

## COAT

### Back

Cast on 16(20, 24, 30) stitches. Work in Garter Stitch until piece measures 6(8, 10, 12) inches from cast on edge.

Decrease 1 stitch at each end of every other row 4(5, 6, 7) times—8(10, 12, 16) stitches remain. Bind off all stitches.

### Front

Cast on 4 stitches. Work 2 rows in Garter Stitch. Beginning on next row, increase 1 stitch at each end every other row 4(6, 9, 12) times to 12(16, 22, 24).

Continue even in Garter Stitch until piece measures 5(6, 8, 10) inches from cast on edge. Bind off all stitches.

## FINISHING

Sew sides of back and front pieces together, leaving a 2(2.5, 3, 3.5) inch area unsewn, where Front begins to get smaller, for the front legs. It can be helpful to measure your dog first, or do a test fitting before sewing the seams.

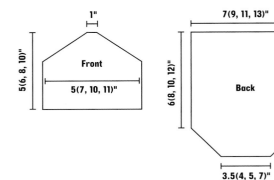

# Fancy Lace Capelet

*By Staceyjoy Elkin*

You're attending a wedding, a garden party, or other dressy occasion and the dog is invited, too. What should she wear? Unless it's a picnic, a bandana is too butch. She deserves to look pretty, and this sweet lace capelet is just the thing. Want to go all out? The ribbon can be color coordinated to match the bridesmaid dresses or your own ensemble.

On the practical side, your dog's everyday collar can be threaded through the neck of the capelet. That way, she can wear her ID and, if necessary, a leash. Just be sure to loosen her collar a bit from its everyday setting. This is a party, after all.

## MATERIALS

* [MC] Crystal Palace Soiree (60% metallic polyester, 40% polyamide; 160 yds per 50 g ball); Color: 3620; 1 ball
* [CC] Karabella Zodiac (100% cotton; 98 yds per 50g ball); Color: Black; 1 ball

* 1 set size US 9/5.5 mm needles for the lace section
* 1 set size US 6/4 mm needles for the collar section

(or sizes needed to match gauge)

* Size F crochet hook

* 1 yard of 1-inch wide velvet ribbon
* Thread to match collar

## GAUGE

**Soiree:** 16 stitches/24 rows = 4 inches in Shark's Tooth

**Zodiac:** 20 stitches/26 rows = 4 inches in Seed Stitch

## TECHNIQUES

### Shark's Tooth Edging

*(The delightfully asymmetrical Shark's Tooth Edging comes from one of Barbara Walker's classic books, A Second Treasury of Knitting Patterns.)*

(8 sts. on needle)

Row 1: Sl 1, k1, (YO, k2tog) twice, YO, k2.
Row 2: K2, YO, k2, (YO, k2tog) twice, k1.
Row 3: Sl 1, k1, (YO, k2tog) twice, k2, YO, k2.
Row 4: K2, YO, k4, (YO, k2tog) twice, k1.
Row 5: Sl 1, k1, (YO, k2tog) twice, k4, YO, k2.
Row 6: K2, YO, k6, (YO, k2tog) twice, k1.
Row 7: Sl 1, k1, (YO, k2tog) twice, k6, YO, k2.
Row 8: K2, YO, k8, (YO, k2tog) twice, k1.
Row 9: Sl 1, k1, (YO, k2tog) twice, k8, YO, k2.
Row 10: K2, YO, k10, (YO, k2tog) twice, k1.
Row 11: Sl 1, k1, (YO, k2tog) twice, k10, YO, k2.
Row 12: BO 11 stitches, k2, (YO, k2tog) twice, k1.

Each repeat of 12 rows equals one shark's tooth.

## SIZE

Finished capelet measures 6 inches from collar to end of lace for all sizes.

**Neck measurement:** 8(10, 12, 16, 20, 24, 28) inches Measure your dog's neck for the most accurate fit.

## CAPELET

Cast on 8 stitches with MC and start Shark's Tooth Edging pattern. Work 5(6, 8, 10, 13, 15, 18) pattern repeats or until the straight edge of the lace measures the same as your dog's neck plus one extra shark's tooth for a tiny dog, two extra shark's teeth for medium size dogs, and three or four extra shark's teeth for a very large dog. If it's too long, it will gather up when attached to the collar. Too short won't be as becoming.

When all shark's teeth are finished: K2tog, k to end of row. Repeat this row until there is 1 stitch left on the needle. Bind off last stitch.

### Collar

With CC, begin at one edge of the lace section (where the yarn tail is), and use crochet hook to pick up and transfer an even number of stitches to knitting needle. Pick up 1 stitch for every row along the straight edge of the collar ending at the other end.

Work in Seed Stitch for 4 rows.

Break off CC. Stitch to MC and [Sl 1 wyib, k1] for 1 row.

[K1, sl 1 wyif] to end of next row. Break off MC.

Switch to CC and work Seed Stitch for 14 rows. Bind off loosely and leave a tail 3 times as long as the collar.

Fold collar section lengthwise into a tube: Thread the long tail onto a yarn needle, and loosely Whipstitch the long edges of the collar together, leaving the short ends open.

Weave in ends. Pin the capelet to the ironing board and steam carefully, placing a damp cloth between the capelet and the iron.

## FINISHING

### Ribbon Ties

Cut the ribbon in half at an angle to prevent unraveling. Place the flat end of ribbon into the collar tube, and stitch it into place from the top of the collar using a sewing needle and thread that matches the collar color. Repeat on the other side.

---

## USE UP YOUR STASH

This capelet is a pretty way to use up small balls of leftover yarn you have on hand. When you're selecting substitutes, choose yarns that knit to a gauge of 4 to 5 stitches per inch for the lace section and one with a suggested gauge of 4 to 5 stitches per inch for the collar section. Note that the collar section is knit on smaller needles than suggested by the yarn manufacturer; the lace section is knit on larger needles for an airy effect.

# Matchy Matchy

Want to wear your puppy love with pride? Then knit up any one of these matching sets. The Irish Fisherdog sweater with matching fingerless gloves will keep both you and your doggy warm and cozy. And you and your pup will be pretty in pink when you don twin Pretty Girl Ponchos. Counterculture types can knit up the Punk Rock collar and matching studded wristband. Is it silly to wear knitwear that matches your dog's? Without a doubt. It's also a whole lot of fun!

* **Feral Fair Isles**
* **Irish Fisherdog and Friend**
* **Pretty Girl Ponchos**
* **Punk Rock Pals**

# Feral Fair Isles
*By Amy Swenson*

This sporty Fair Isle sweater and hat set looks chic on even the most domesticated dogs and their humans. Knit in modern neutrals, the colors work well for both boys and girls. The color sections are constrained to the yoke and hem of the sweater and the border of the hat. The rest is easy-going, single color stockinette. If you've never worked with two-stranded knitting, these small projects are a great way to experiment and gain experience.

## MATERIALS

* Mission Falls 1824 Wool (100% superwash wool; 85 m per 50g skein):
  [MC] Color: 001 (Natural); 3(3, 4, 5) skeins
  [CC1] Color: 007 (Cocoa); 1(1, 2, 2) skeins
  [CC2] Color: 010 (Russet); 1(1, 1, 1) skeins
  [CC3] Color: 028 (Pistachio); 1(1, 1, 1) skeins

Yarn quantities include enough for one sweater and one hat. If knitting only the hat, you'll need 1 ball in each color.

* 1 set US 5/3.75 mm DPNs
* 1 16-inch long US 5/3.75 mm circular needle
* 1 16-inch long US 7/4.5 mm circular needle
* 1 spare US 7/4.5 mm needle, any length
(or sizes needed to match gauge)

* Stitch holder
* Stitch markers

## GAUGE

18 stitches/24 rows = 4 inches in Stockinette Stitch on US 7/4.5 mm needles

## SIZE

**Dog sweater**
**Chest:** 16(20, 24, 28) inches around
**Sweater length:** 12(14, 16, 18) inches

**Pom-pom hat**
One size fits most

## SWEATER

With smaller circular needle and CC1, cast on 40(48, 56, 64) stitches. Place marker and join to begin working in the rounds. Work k1, p1 rib for 6 rounds.

On next round, switch to larger circular needle and knit to 1 stitch before end of round, m1, place marker, k1, m1. 42(50, 58, 66) stitches. The 2 stitches between the markers are the beginning of the belly of the sweater.

## MAKING IT FIT

Due to the chart-based pattern, this sweater is a bit tricky to customize to your dog's exact measurements. If you alter the neck and chest measurements, make sure to add stitches to the back panel in multiples of four to maintain the integrity of the chart pattern. To increase the length, simply add additional rows to the white stockinette portion of the sweater before beginning the color work on the hem. If you increase the length after casting off at the belly, remember to pick up additional stitches on each side of the back before working the ribbed edging.

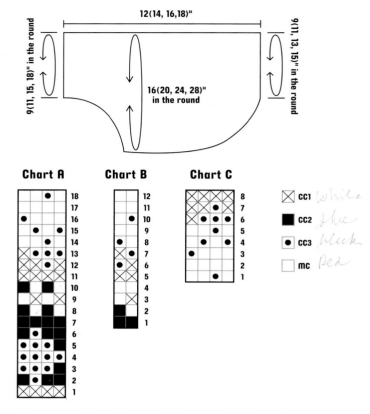

12(14, 16, 18)"

9(11, 15, 18)" in the round

9(11, 13, 15)" in the round

16(20, 24, 28)" in the round

**Chart A**    **Chart B**    **Chart C**

⊠ CC1  *white*

■ CC2  *blue*

● CC3  *black*

□ MC  *Red*

On next round, work Row 1 of Chart A, increasing as follows: Work Chart A as directed to first marker. Slip marker, m1, k2, m1, slip marker at end of round. Increase 2 stitches between markers by working m1 increases after first marker and before second marker every row for 2-6(2-6, 2-10, 2-14) of Chart A. 54(62, 78, 94) stitches.

Between markers, simply alternate working colors.

Next row: Work Chart A as established to first marker. Place next 14(14, 22, 30) stitches on holder and set aside.

Turn work, and work ring side-to-side, work remaining rows of Chart A over the remaining 40(48, 56, 64) live stitches.

In pattern, increase 1 stitch at each end of needle every RS row 0(0, 3, 5) times. 40(48, 62, 74) stitches.

After finishing Chart A, work 1(1, 3, 5) row(s) even in MC and set aside.

With spare needle, pick up 14(14, 22, 30) held stitches and work following Chart B. Increase 1 stitch at each end of needle every row for 6(6, 8, 10) rows to 26(26, 38, 50) stitches. After finishing Chart B, work 1(1, 3, 5) row(s) even in MC and set aside.

Pick up body again and k across all 40(48, 62, 74) stitches with MC. Place marker and pick up held front stitches. K across 26(26, 38, 50) held stitches with MC, place marker. On next round and every other round 0(0, 2, 2) times, increase as follows: K1, m1, k to 1 stitch before marker, m1, k1, slip marker, k1, m1, k to 1 stitch before marker, m1, k1.

When all increases are complete, you'll have 42(50, 68, 80) stitches between one set of markers and 28(28, 44, 56) stitches between the other two markers for a total of 70(78, 112, 136) stitches.

Continue in Stockinette Stitch until piece measures 7(9, 11, 13) inches from cast on edge.

On next round, k to 7(7, 10, 13) stitches past first marker. Bind off next 14(14, 20, 26) stitches, k to end. 56(64, 92, 110) stitches remain.

Turn work and purl 1 row.
Bind off 3 stitches at beginning of next 2 rows. 50(58, 86, 100) stitches remain.
Bind off 2 stitches at beginning of next 2 rows. 46(54, 82, 96) stitches remain.
Decrease 1 stitch at each end of next 2(2, 3, 4) RS rows. 42(50, 76, 88) stitches remain.
Purl 1 row.
Work Rows 1-8 of Chart C.

Work rows 1-7 of Chart C. After finishing Row 7, do not bind off. Instead, continue around side of dog sweater as follows.
With A, pick up and knit 20(20, 22, 24) stitches along left side edge. Pick up and knit 14(14, 20, 26) stitches along bottom, pick up and knit 20(20, 22, 24) stitches along right side edge, join to beginning.

Switch to smaller circular needle or DPNs and continue in rounds. Work 6 rounds k1, p1 rib in A. Cast off in rib.

### Armholes

With A and smaller gauge DPNs, and with right side facing, pick up and knit 30(30, 36, 40) stitches along armhole. Work 6 rounds k1, p1 rib. Cast off in rib.

### POM-POM HAT

With smaller circular needle and CC1, cast on 88 stitches, place marker and join to begin working in the round. Work k1, p1 rib for 6 rounds.

Switch to larger circular needles; knit 1 round even. Beginning with Row 1 of Chart A, continue to work Chart A as indicated for next 18 rounds.

Switch to MC and continue in Stockinette Stitch until hat measures 6 inches from cast on edge.

[K2tog, k6] 11 times. (77 stitches)
Knit 4 rounds even.
[K2tog, k5] 11 times. (66 stitches)
Knit 3 rounds even.
[K2tog, k4] 11 times. (55 stitches)
Knit 2 rounds even.
[K2tog, k3] 11 times. (44 stitches)
Knit 1 round even.
[K2tog, k2] 11 times. (33 stitches)
Knit 1 round even.
[K2tog, k1] 11 times. (22 stitches)
[K2tog] 11 times. (11 stitches)
Cut yarn, thread through remaining stitches, and pull tight.

Weave in ends and steam-block if desired.

Using leftover yarn in your choice of colors, wrap yarn around a matchbook or small square of cardboard 100 times. Using a yarn needle, pull a 2-foot length of yarn through the loops of yarn several times, pull tightly and knot to secure. Cut loops opposite of tied end and trim to form pom-pom shape. Attach to top of hat.

# Irish Fisherdog and Friend
*By Amy Swenson*

Any dog will look just dashing in this modern version of a traditional cabled Irish Fisherman sweater. Knit with bulky wool, this heirloom sweater is a speedy introduction to cables. The neck and tail ends are left unribbed for an updated look on an old favorite. The Seed-Stitch panels on the side are more than an attractive feature; they allow the sweater to be knit with or without sleeves, while still maintaining a finished appearance. And don't forget the matching fingerless gloves for you! The bulky cables are a nod to the Aran Islands where the style originated, while the fingerless design allows you to hold your pup's leash with ease.

## MATERIALS

### Dog sweater

* Brown Sheep Lamb's Pride Bulky (85% Wool, 15% mohair; 125 yds per 113g skein); Color: M115 Oatmeal; 2(2, 2, 3, 3) skeins
* 1 set US 8/5 mm DPNs
* 1 set US 10/6 mm needles

### Fingerless gloves

* same yarn specified above, 2 skeins
* 5 US 10/6 mm DPNs
  (or size necessary to match gauge)

## GAUGE

12 stitches/16 rows = 4 inches
in Stockinette Stitch on larger needles

## TECHNIQUES

**4-Stitch Right Cable:** Slip 2 stitches to cable needle and hold to back of work. K2, k2 from cable needle.

**4-Stitch Left Cable:** Slip 2 stitches to cable needle and hold to front of work. K2, k2 from cable needle.

**6-Stitch Right Cable:** Slip 3 stitches to cable needle and hold to back of work. K3, k3 from cable needle.

**6-Stitch Left Cable:** Slip 3 stitches to cable needle and hold to front of work. K3, k3 from cable needle.

**Decrease while binding off:** To decrease over a cable while binding off, k1, k2tog, pull first stitch over decreased stitch to bind off.

## SIZE

### Dog sweater

**Chest:** 20(24, 28, 32, 38) inches
**Back length:** 12(16, 20, 24, 28) inches

(To customize the sweater for your dog's unique shape and size, pick the chest measurement that works best, then alter the length of both pieces to fit. If altering the length, determine the desired back length first, then find the appropriate front length by subtracting four inches.)

### Fingerless gloves

One size fits most

## SWEATER

### Back

With larger needles, cast on 30(36, 42, 48, 54) stitches. Work in Seed Stitch for 1(4, 7, 10, 13) stitches, work Chart A over 8 stitches, work Chart B over 12 stitches, work Chart C over 8 stitches, work Seed Stitch to end.

Continue in this way, working in the pattern established.

Beginning on the fifth row, increase 1 stitch on each edge. Repeat increases every other right side(RS) row 4(5, 6, 7, 8) times: 40(48, 56, 64, 73) stitches.

Work even in pattern until Back measures 12(16, 20, 24, 28) inches from cast on edge.

Bind off, decreasing 1 stitch in Panel A, 3 stitches in Panel B, and 1 stitch in Panel C.

### Front

With larger needles, cast on 16(20, 24, 28, 32) stitches. Work Seed Stitch for 0(2, 4, 6, 8) stitches, p2, work Chart B over 12 stitches, p2, work Seed Stitch for 2 stitches.

Beginning on next RS row, increase 1 stitch on each edge. Repeat increases on next 5(7, 9, 11, 13) RS rows. 28(36, 44, 52, 60) stitches.

Continue even in pattern until Front measures 8(12, 16, 19, 23) inches from cast on edge.

Bind off, decreasing 3 stitches in panel B.

### Chart A

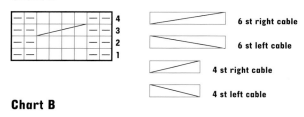

```
                              6 st right cable

                              6 st left cable

                              4 st right cable

                              4 st left cable
```

### Chart B

### Chart C

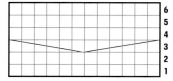

## DON'T SHRINK YOUR WOOL!

Brown Sheep Lamb's Pride Bulky is a wool/mohair single-ply yarn and available in a virtual rainbow of colors. The stitch definition is nice, and the mohair content provides a nice comforting halo of fuzz to the finished work. However, it is decidedly not machine washable! So, hand wash the final sweater and gloves, or be prepared for shrinkage! If easy care is a priority, look for a bulky yarn that's advertised as machine washable.

## FINISHING

Beginning at neck, sew Front to Back, leaving a 2.25(2.5, 3, 3.5, 4) inch area unattached for armhole. (The seams add some additional circumference to the armhole.)

This is a great time to do a quick fitting, as you can adjust the position and size of the armholes based on your dog's unique shape. Before knitting on the sleeves, use pins to assemble the sweater with armholes in place and put the piece on your dog. If your dog's shoulders are more or less stocky than accounted for in the pattern, you may need to open or close the armholes a little before picking up the sleeve stitches.

Remember, if you do alter the arm holes, change the number of sleeve stitches as follows: Measure the circumference of the armhole in inches and multiply by three to determine how many stitches you'll need to pick up along the edge of the armhole. Round to an even number. The pattern assumes an armhole circumference of 6(7, 8, 9, 11) inches.

### Arms

If ribbing around the armholes is desired, use the smaller DPNs to pick up and knit 18(20, 24, 28, 32) stitches around the armhole. Work 5(5, 5, 7, 7) rows in k1, p1 rib. Bind off in rib.

## GLOVES

**With DPNs cast on 22 stitches, dividing over 4 needles as follows: 5 stitches, 5 stitches, 6 stitches, 6 stitches. Place marker and join.

Work Chart D over first 2 needles, increasing 1 stitch at end of first needle, and 1 stitch at beginning of 2nd needle. Work Seed Stitch over 12 stitches on 3rd and 4th needles.

Work Rows 1-6 of Chart D 3 times, then Rows 1-2 of Chart D.**

### Right Hand Shaping

On next row, work Chart E, m1 purlwise, work Chart F, work Seed Stitch for 2 stitches. Turn work and continue in pattern, working side to side.

Work 3 more rows as established, then increase 1 stitch purlwise between Chart F and Chart E on fourth row. Repeat increase every fourth row 2 more times (28 stitches on needles).

On next RS row, work Charts and 2 Seed Stitch edge stitches as established, then continue working in the round, joining with the palm side in Seed Stitch. Continue in patterns as set for 5 more rounds.

Bind off, decreasing 1 stitch in each cable panel.

### Left Hand Shaping

Work ** to ** on previous page. On next row, work Chart F, m1 purlwise, work Chart E, work Seed Stitch until 2 stitches before end of round. Turn work and continue in pattern, working side to side.

Work 3 rows as established, then increase 1 stitch purlwise between Chart F and Chart E on fourth row. Repeat increase every fourth row 2 more times. (28 stitches on needles).

On next RS row, work Charts and continue with Seed Stitch to end of round, then continue working in the round, joining with the palm side in Seed Stitch. Continue as patterned for 5 more rounds.

Bind off, decreasing 1 stitch in each cable panel.

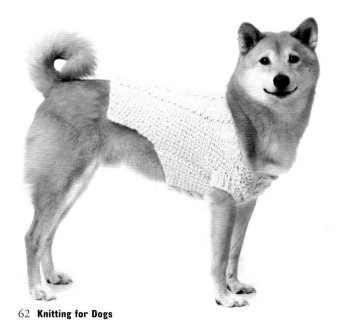

Sew in ends and lightly block, if desired. Dress your dog in his sweater. Don your gloves, and go for a matchy-matchy walk!

### Chart D

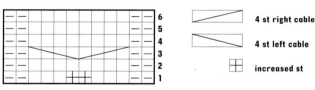

|  |  | 4 st right cable |
|--|--|------------------|
|  |  | 4 st left cable |
|  |  | increased st |

### Chart E

### Chart F

# Pretty Girl Ponchos

*By Heather Brack*

A girl and her best four-legged friend are bound to turn heads walking down the street in these bright matching ponchos. The unique mesh-tape yarn is super bulky but extremely lightweight, providing just a little extra warmth on a chilly evening. Because they're knit on the bias, these ponchos drape gracefully and have a unique asymmetrical shape that can be worn many ways. The four sizes given here will fit dogs of all sizes—from a Yorkie to Mastiff. The two smallest sizes will fit medium or large dogs, the two largest sizes will fit children (the human kind) and adults. How's that for sharing?

## MATERIALS

* Crystal Palace Big Net (40% polyamide, 30% wool, 30% acrylic; 88 yds per 100 g skein); Color: 3676; 2(2, 4, 5) skeins

* 1 set US 17/12 mm needles (or size to match gauge)

## GAUGE

Approximately 7 stitches/10 rows = 4 inches (this is a very stretchy fabric)

## SIZES: human and dog

**Approximate length at longest point:**
8(13, 18, 23) inches
**Neck opening:** 10(20, 30, 40) inches around

Choose sizes based on the length, because it's especially important that your dog not trip over the fringe. The width of the neck opening can be adjusted by extending the seams on one or both sides.

## PONCHO

(Knit 2 pieces the same)

Cast on 1 stitch.

### Increase section

Row 1: K1fb.
Row 2 and all even rows: Purl across.
Row 3: K1fb, k1.
Row 5: K1fb, k1fb, k1.
Row 7: K1fb, k to 2 stitches from end, k1fb, k1.
Row 8: Purl.

Repeat rows 7 and 8 until there are 9(25, 29, 35) stitches on the needle.

## Straight section

Row 1(RS): K1fb, k to 3 stitches from end of row, k2tog, k1.

Row 2: Purl all stitches.

Repeat these two rows until the longer edge measures 10(20, 30, 40) inches.

## Decrease section

Row 1 (RS): K1, k2tog, k to 3 stitches from end of row, k2tog, k1.

Row 2: Purl all stitches.

Repeat these two rows until 5 stitches remain.

Next RS row: K1, k2tog, k2.

Next row: Purl all stitches.

Next row: K2tog twice.

Next row: Purl all stitches.

Next row: K2tog.

Break yarn and pull through last stitch.

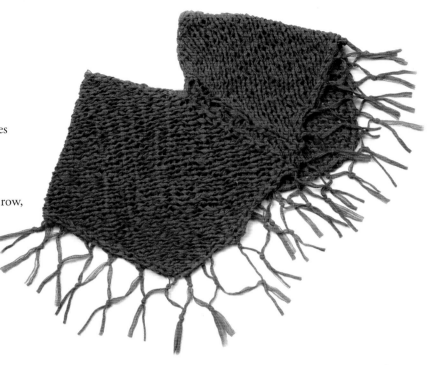

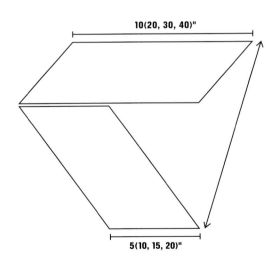

10(20, 30, 40)"

5(10, 15, 20)"

Line up the short edge of one piece along the long edge of the other piece as shown with right sides together. Stitch together loosely. Repeat at opposite end.

Try on and lengthen seams to adjust neckline as necessary.

### Fringe

Cut lengths of fringe about 10-inches long from remaining yarn. Loop fringe lengths in half and insert through a stitch, pulling the two ends through the top of the loop to secure. Attach a length of fringe to every 3rd stitch. Knot adjacent strands of fringe together as shown in photographs.

# Punk Rock Pals

*By Heather Brack*

Even though they knit up in practically no time, these studded and rhinestoned collars and matching wristbands are definitely not short on style. Knit them in the colors shown, or dive into your stash and make a funky multi-colored creation with your wool scraps. Wanna wear a dog collar, too? Rock on.

Most craft or fabric stores will have two different kinds of snaps—one that attaches with a special set of pliers and another that has to be set with a hammer. The pliers are more expensive but much easier to use.

## MATERIALS

* Cascade 220 (100% wool; 220 yds per 100g skein); Color: 8555 Black or 8422 Tibetan Rose; 1 skein
* 1 set US 10/6 mm needles
* Studs, grommets, or rhinestones with prong settings
* 2 4-piece snaps and setting tool (available at sewing and craft stores)

## GAUGE

16 stitches/20 rows = 4 inches in Garter Stitch before felting
Gauge need not be exact and finished collars will shrink when felted.

## SIZE

**Finished width (collar):** 1(1.5) inches
**Finished width (wristband):** 1(1.5) inches

## COLLAR / WRISTBAND

Measure your dog's regular collar on your wrist and multiply the result by 1.5. This number will be the pre-felting length of your knitted collar.

Cast on 5(8) stitches for collar or wristband, and knit in Garter Stitch until you've reached the length calculated above.

Bind off loosely.

### Felting

If you were to try to felt a long strip of wool in the washing machine, you'd probably just end up with a tangled mess. The best way to make sure your collar keeps its shape is to felt it by hand in the sink.

Fill a sink or a large bowl with hot water (as hot as you can comfortably plunge your hands into), and add a squirt of dish soap or liquid hand soap.

Roll the collar or wristband tightly from one end to the other and submerge it in the water until it is soaked all the way through, then squeeze and roll it between the palms of your hands. The stitches will first seem to stretch out, then will begin to shrink and stick together. Periodically

## FELTING BASICS

Any feltable wool yarn can be substituted in this pattern. Some suggestions include Brown Sheep Lamb's Pride, Manos Del Uruguay, or Auracania Nature Wool. To test if your yarn will felt, roll a small piece into a ball in hot soapy water. If the ball holds together so you can't pull the strand straight again, your yarn is felting. Try using these test balls as beads or buttons.

unroll the collar to check your progress, then roll it back up from the other end so that it felts evenly. Keep going until it's a solid strip of fabric and the individual stitches are almost invisible. This may take 15 to 30 minutes.

### FINISHING

After felting, your collar or wristband should be roughly 3 inches longer than your dog's neck or your wrist measurement. If it's longer than this and you're satisfied with the extent of the felting, you can trim it with scissors, the fabric should not fray or unravel.

Lay out your studs flat on the collar or wristband. You can use the photos as a guide or make up your own pattern. Leave 1.5 inches on one end and 3 inches on the other end unadorned so that you have room to attach the snaps. Once you have the pattern planned, set the studs. If you happen to have a BeDazzler or other rhinestone setting tool, this step will be a breeze. If you don't, there's no need to buy one just for this project. You can set the studs by hand by pressing the prongs on the back through the fabric and bending them toward the center. They should bend easily, but you can use any tool you have handy to help—the side of your scissors, a butter knife, or a screwdriver.

Finally, place the snaps. To make the collar adjustable, in case your dog grows or goes through a crazy-hair phase, place one snap bottom 0.5 inches and another snap bottom 2 inches from one end of the collar. Set the top of the snap 0.5 inches from the other side, being sure to place snaps so they connect without twisting the collar.

# Accessories Make the Dog

Too many rawhide bones, pet squeakers, and stuffed animals cluttering your domestic landscape? Your dog's many accoutrements are part of your shared space, so why not make some you'll actually enjoy seeing? Here you'll find patterns for all sorts of great gear, including an adorable bed, an herbal flea collar, and a selection of toys to play with.

* Dog Napper
* Sweet Potato Chain
* Cat Squeaker
* I ♥ My Bone
* New Age Flea Collar
* Walk in the Park Bag
* "Get Along Little Doggy" Saddlebag
* Disco Dog Legwarmers

# Dog Napper

*By Amy Swenson*

This easy bed, knit on big needles from a thick acrylic-wool blend, can be completed in a weekend. The lovely textured pattern keeps it interesting and also provides a tight gauge to keep the stuffing from poking out. The bed is also tufted in five places to create a more tailored look and help maintain the bed's shape. It's made from a washable blend that can be thrown in the washing machine for easy cleaning.

Three sizes are provided below. Make sure the bed is long enough for your dog to stretch out on. (If your dog is a puppy, you may need to knit a larger size as she grows!) Alternatively, knit this napper to fit the dimensions of her kennel to make car rides more comfortable.

## MATERIALS

* Lion Brand Wool-Ease Thick & Quick (80% Acrylic, 20% Wool; 106 yds per 170g skein); Color: 131 Grass; 3(5, 8) skeins

* 1 set US 13/9 mm needles (or size needed to match gauge)

* Polyester fiberfill

## GAUGE

9 stitches/12 rows to 4 inches in Stockinette Stitch

## TECHNIQUES

**Woven Stitch**

Row 1: K1 [slip 1 stitch with yarn in front, k1] across
Row 2: K2, [slip 1 stitch with yarn in front, k1] across

## SIZE

**Width:** 17(24, 31) inches
**Length:** 21(28, 35) inches

### BED

Cast on 43(61, 77) stitches and purl 1 row.
Work Rows 1 and 2 of Woven Stitch until piece is 21(28, 35) inches long, or as desired. Bind off all stitches.

Make second panel the same.

### FINISHING

Sew two pieces together, leaving a hole for the stuffing. Stuff as desired and sew closed.

With yarn needle and spare yarn, insert needle at center of bed from Back to Front. Sew bed together by passing the needle back and forth several times. Pull tight and secure ends. Repeat at four points equidistant from the four corners of the bed using the photo as a guide.

# Sweet Potato Chain

*By Staceyjoy Elkin*

This sweet potato-shaped amusement doubles as a soft little sculpture that won't compete with your home décor (although it will be covered in slobber most of the time). Strong enough to survive some serious tug of war with smaller dogs, this toy has the added advantage of squeaking piteously in three separate places! For very small dogs, you can stop knitting after one potato; for large dogs, why not knit five spuds, and stitch the ends together to make a ring?

## MATERIALS

* Artful Yarns Dance (50% cotton, 50% Acrylic; 70 yds per 100g skein); 1 skein (2 skeins for a five-spud version)

* 4 size US 9/5.5 mm DPNs (or size needed to match gauge)

* Large yarn needle

* Polyester fiberfill for stuffing
* 3 small dime-store squeaky toys, or replacement squeakers

## GAUGE

12 stitches/18 rows = 4 inches in Stockinette Stitch.

## TOY

Cast on 9 stitches, 3 on each of 3 needles. The fourth needle is the working needle. Leave a 10-inch tail.

Join, and k 1 round.

## ONE POTATO

Round 1: [K2, m1, k1] 3 times,
Round 2 and all even rows: Knit.
Round 3: [K3, m1, k1] 3 times.
Round 5: [K4, m1, k1] 3 times.

Continue increasing as set until there are 9 stitches on each needle. Knit 1 round.

Turn the work inside out, thread the 10-inch tail on a large yarn needle, and run the yarn through the stitches on the edge. Pull tight to close, run the yarn through the stitches once more, turn and run it through in the opposite direction a few stitches to lock it in, and cut. Turn work right side out again.

## Stuffing

Place a firm layer of stuffing against the inside edges of the knitting. Leave space in the middle for the squeaker.

## Decreasing

Decreases are worked every round.
Round 1: [K2tog, k7] 3 times.
Round 2: [K2tog, k6] 3 times.
Round 3: [K2tog, k5] 3 times.

Wrap the squeaker completely in stuffing, and place it in the spud. Fill any void with stuffing.
Round 4: [K2tog, k4] 3 times.
Round 5: [K2tog, k3] 3 times.

Check stuffing level. Top up if needed.
Round 6: [K2tog, k2] 3 times.
Round 7: [K2tog, k1] 3 times—
2 stitches on each needle.

Knit 2 rounds on the 6 stitches.

## YARN NOTES

You can substitute another yarn: a tightly spun cotton, linen, acrylic, or any blend of the three would work best. For "forgotten potato at back of fridge" fuzz, mix an eyelash yarn in with some cotton. To create a tight knit, the needles are two sizes smaller than the size recommended for the yarn. That way, the toy can withstand your dog's perpetual chewing and mouthing action without losing its stuffing.

### TWO POTATO

**Increasing**

Round 1: [K1, m1, k1] 3 times.
Round 2 and all even rounds: Knit.
Round 3: [K2, m1, k1] 3 times.
Round 5: [K3, m1, k1] 3 times.
Round 7: [K4, m1, k1] 3 times.

Continue increasing like this until there are 9 stitches on each needle, and knit 1 round.
Stuff the same way as the first spud.

**Decreasing**

Round 1: [K2tog, k7] 3 times.
Round 2 and all even rounds: Knit.
Round 3: [K2tog, k6] 3 times.
Round 5: [K2tog, k5] 3 times.

Add stuffing-wrapped squeaker.
Round 7: [K2tog, k4] 3 times.
Round 9: [K2tog, k3] 3 times.

Check stuffing level. Fill if needed.

Round 11: [K2tog, k2] 3 times.
Round 13: [K2tog, k1] 3 times. 2 stitches on each needle.

Knit 2 rounds on the 6 stitches.

### THREE POTATO

**Increasing**

Increases are worked every round.
Round 1: [K1, m1, k1] 3 times.
Round 2: [K2, m1, k1] 3 times.
Round 3: [K3, m1, k1] 3 times.
Round 4: [K4, m1, k1] 3 times.

Continue increasing like this until there are 9 stitches on each needle, then knit 1 round.
Stuff spud.

**Decreasing**

Round 1: [K2tog, k7] 3 times.
Round 2 and all even rounds: Knit.
Round 3: [K2tog, k6] 3 times.

Add squeaker. You know the drill.

Round 5: [K2tog, k5] 3 times.
Round 7: [K2tog, k4] 3 times.
Round 9: [K2tog, k3] 3 times.

Check stuffing level. Fill if needed.
Round 11: [K2tog, k2] 3 times. (9 stitches, 3 on each needle.)
Round 12: Knit.
Cut, leaving a 10-inch tail.

**FINISHING**

Using yarn needle, thread tail through remaining stitches a few times and weave ends in very securely.

# Cat Squeaker

*By Amy Swenson*

This adorable stuffed squeaky cat will give your dog hours of vindictive pleasure. Knit in pieces and quickly stitched together, this project can be completed in a single evening. While most of the cat is made of simple Stockinette squares, the head features short-row shaping to create the ears.

Stuff in a small, smooth squeaker so you'll know what your dog is up to.

## MATERIALS

* Lang Tosca (55% wool, 45% acrylic; 100 yds per 50g skein); Color: 60; 1 skein

* 1 set US 6/4 mm DPNs
* 1 set US 6/4 mm needles

(or size needed to match gauge)

* 2-inch or smaller squeaky toy, or replacement squeaker
* Polyester fiberfill

## GAUGE

20 stitches/26 rows = 4 inches in Stockinette Stitch on US 6/4 mm needles

(recommended gauge for yarn used is 12 stitches/ 17 rows = 4 inches in Stockinette Stitch on US 10.5/6.5 mm needles)

## TECHNIQUES

**W+T (Wrap and Turn)** Used to create tidy shortrows. (See below)

**On right side of work:** Bring yarn to front of work, and slip next stitch. Turn work, slip wrapped stitch to right needle and bring yarn to working side.

**On wrong side of work:** Hold yarn to back of work and slip next stitch. Turn work, slip wrapped stitch to right needle and bring yarn to working side.

## SIZE

Approximately 12-inches high and 7-inches wide, from paw to paw.

## PATTERN

### Body (make 2)
Cast on 18 stitches. Work in Stockinette Stitch until piece is 5.5-inches long. Bind off.

### Arms (make 2)
Cast on 8 stitches. Work in Stockinette Stitch until 6-inches long. Bind off.

### Legs (make 2)
Cast on 8 stitches. Work in Stockinette Stitch until 8-inches long. Bind off.

**Head (make 1)**

Cast on 12 stitches. Work 2 rows in Stockinette Stitch. Beginning on next RS row, increase 1 stitch on each end of row. Work increases in this way on next 2 RS rows. (18 stitches). Continue in Stockinette Stitch until piece measures 3.5 inches from cast on edge.

K5, w+t, p5.

K5, w+t, p5.

K4, w+t, p4.

K3, w+t, p3.

K3, pick up wrap and place on left needle, knit together with slipped stitch. W+t, p4.

K4, pick up two wraps and place on left needle, knit them together with slipped stitch. W+t, p5.

K5, pick up 3 wraps and place on left needle, knit them together with slipped stitch. K to end.

Turn work. Repeat short row shaping as follows:

P5, w+t, k5.

P5, w+t, k5.

P4, w+t, k4.

P3, w+t, k3.

P3, pick up wrap and place on left needle, purl together with slipped stitch. W+t, k4.

P4, pick up two wraps and place on left needle, knit them together with slipped stitch. W+t, k5.

P5, pick up 3 wraps and place on left needle, knit them together with slipped stitch. P to end.

Continue working in Stockinette Stitch until piece measures 5.5 inches from cast on edge. On next RS row, decrease 1 stitch each edge of work. Decrease in this way every RS row two more times. (12 stitches remain). Work 2 rows even in Stockinette Stitch. Bind off.

**FINISHING**

Fold arm in half to create a 3-inch long pouch. Sew sides, leaving small hole for stuffing. Stuff as desired and sew closed. Repeat with other arm and with both legs.

Sew two body panels together, leaving small hole. Stuff with Polyester fiberfill and squeaker, and sew closed.

Fold head in half so ears are at top. Sew sides, leaving neck open. Stuff and sew closed.

Sew head to top of body. When attaching pieces, you'll get a more secure seam if you sew both sides of the head to the body. Stuff as desired and finish seaming.

Sew legs and arms to body in the same way.

Secure any loose ends by pulling through the body stuffing a few times and cutting.

**Tail**

With DPNs, pick up 4 stitches along back edge of body to form the base of the tail. Work in icord for 9 inches. Cut yarn and pull through stitches to fasten. Tie knot in end of tail. Secure any loose ends.

## GET YOUR GAUGE ON

This kitty is constructed from small squares of Lang Tosca, a yarn that gradually shifts color, creating a nifty patchwork effect. We give the gauge recommended by the manufacturer in the Gauge section of this pattern. If substituting yarns, remember to use one with the manufacturer's suggested gauge. The toy is then knit on much smaller needles to create a tight knit so the stuffing won't seep through the stitches!

# I ♥ My Bone

*By Amy Swenson*

This durable chew toy is a great homemade gift that looks a lot like commercial rope bones sold in pet stores. Knit with Poly Utility Cord, easily found in your local hardware store, it's a quick project that can be completed in one evening.

Three sizes are provided, but this pattern makes it a cinch to improvise. Knit the bone as long or as short as you like; just remember to leave room for the knots at the ends. Is your cord thicker than the one specified? Great! You'll end up with a thicker bone your pup can really sink his teeth into.

## MATERIALS

* Poly Utility Cord (100% polyacrylic, ³⁄₁₆-inch thick); 15(60, 100) yds

* 1 set US 13/9 mm DPNs (or size needed to match gauge)
* Yarn needle

## GAUGE

12 stitches/16 rows = 4 inches in Stockinette Stitch

## SIZE

**Length:** 6(12, 14) inches

## TOY

With DPNs, cast on 3(4, 5) stitches.
(For sizes M and L, make 3 pieces the same.)

## Work icord as follows

*K(3, 3, 4) stitches, but do not turn needle.
Slide stitches to right end of needle.*

Repeat from * to * until cord is 12(26, 32) inches long. Cut cord and pull through stitches to fasten off. Weave end down into body of icord.

## FINISHING

For S only, take single cord and work a knot at each end. For M and L, braid three cords together and tie with a knot at each end.

# New Age Flea Collar

*By Staceyjoy Elkin*

This collar is a pleasant-smelling herbal alternative to stinky commercial flea collars made with harsh chemicals. It's filled with dried pennyroyal, thyme, and wormwood, a time-honored mixture with natural flea-repellant properties. Because the herbs need to be fresh, these collars are not washable or refillable. You'll need to make a new one each season. If your dog is exposed to fleas frequently (walks in the woods will do it), try treating this collar with essential oils, too. Just take off the treated collar when you get home, before your dog settles down on your favorite armchair.

## MATERIALS

* Schachenmayr Nomotta Crazy Cotton (100% cotton; 137 yds per 50g ball); Color: 86; 1 ball
Or
* Schachenmayr Nomotta Catania Color (100% cotton; 137 yds per 50g ball); Color: 75; 1 ball

* 1 set US 3/3.25 mm needles
(or size needed to match gauge)

* Two 3/4-inch D-rings
* Herbs: 2 parts pennyroyal, 1 part thyme, 1 part wormwood—mixed together.

## GAUGE

30 stitches/36 rows = 4 inches in DK

## TECHNIQUES

With two needles, you'll knit seamless little pockets and stuff them halfway full with the herbal mixture before knitting the pockets shut. The herbs will flatten out a bit (the pockets should look like raviolis). If your knitting tension is not tight enough to keep the herbs inside, use a smaller needle.

## SIZE

**Neck measurement:** 8(10, 12, 16, 20, 24, 28)

## COLLAR

Cast on 8 stitches.
Row 1: Sl 1, k7. Repeat this row 14 times.

Slide knitting through the 2 D-rings and close the loop:
Pick up 1 stitch from cast on edge and ktog with 1 stitch
on needle. Repeat to end of row. K1 row.

Next row: k1fb 3 times, (k1fb, then k into front of stitch
again) twice, k1fb 3 times. 18 stitches.

**Start Pocket (DK):
Work [k1, sl 1 wyib] to end of row. Repeat 20 times.

### YARNS AND CHARMS

If you substitute yarns, stick with cotton, bamboo, or
linen. Going up in gauge is not recommended, as the
collar will get too heavy for comfort. The pit bull
charms shown in the photos were found in a super-
market vending machine, but you can hang a small
charm of your own choosing for extra mojo.

### Stuff Pocket

[Sl 1 stitch to RH needle, Sl 1 stitch to 3rd needle]
7 times. You'll have 7 stitches on RH needle, 7 stitches
on 3rd needle and 4 stitches on LH needle and an open
pocket. Carefully spoon in a half-pocketful of herbs.
Return stitches to LH needle in reverse order of removal.

### Close Pocket

[K2, sl 1 wyib] to end of row. Repeat once.** One pocket
complete!

Repeat ** to ** 4(5, 6, 8, 10, 12, 14) times.

After knitting and sealing the last pocket: K2tog 3 times,
[sl 1, k2tog, psso] 2 times, k2tog 3 times. 8 stitches
remain.

Next row: Sl 1, k7. Repeat this row for 3 inches.

[K2tog, k to end of row] for 7 rows. Bind off last stitch.

### FINISHING

Weave in ends. Your dog is ready for the great outdoors!

# Walk in the Park Bag
*By Staceyjoy Elkin*

This handy bag is designed with enough compartments to hold everything you need for a morning walk in the park—small things like lipstick and coffee money, plus essentials like treats, water, keys, and plastic bags. Prepack it at night so you can grab it as your dog drags you out the front door. Be sure to attach an extra set of keys to the bag, and you'll never get locked out of your house wearing nothing but pajama pants and a T-shirt in the rain. Hey, it happens.

## MATERIALS

* Tahki Classic (100% Mercerized Cotton; 108 yds per 50g hank); Colors: 3786 Teal, 3725 Avocado Green, 3805 Light Turquoise; 1 hank of each color.

* 1 set size US 5/3.5 mm needles
* 1 16-inch length US 6/4 mm circular needle
* 1 size US 6/4 mm DPNs
(or sizes needed to match gauge)

* Size F crochet

* Two 1.5 inch square metal rings

## GAUGE

22 stitches/28 rows = 4 inches in Stockinette Stitch

## TECHNIQUES

**Decrease bind-off** [K2tog, sl stitch back to left needle]—Repeat to end of row.

**Three-needle bind-off** With 2 right-side pieces facing each other, hold 2 needles parallel in the left hand and insert a third needle into first stitch on the first needle and then through the first stitch on the second needle. Knit these two stitches together as one. Knit the second stitch on each needle together as one. Slip the first stitch on the third needle over the second stitch to bind off. Continue in this way, to the end of the row or as instructed in the pattern.

## SIZE

One size does the job.

## BAG

### Pockets Side

Using Teal and smaller needles, cast on 54 stitches. Begin DK: [K1, sl 1 wyib] across. Repeat this row 19 times.

*Row 21: DK 10 stitches. Cut yarn with a 10-inch tail and tie on yards of yarn. DK in waste yarn for 34 stitches. Cut waste yarn and reattach Teal, DK to end of row (10 stitches).*

DK 5 more rows.

Change color to Avocado. Next 2 rows are sealing rows: **K2, [Sl 1, k1] to end of row. Work next row the same.**

DK 14 rows. Make another opening with waste yarn (repeat * to * above), then DK 4 more rows in Avocado.

Change to Light Turquoise and seal second opening (repeat ** to ** above).

DK 14 rows (Light Turquoise). Make another opening with waste yarn (repeat * to *), then DK 4 more rows in Light Turquoise.

Use Decrease Bind-off (see above) to finish Pockets section.

## Pouch Side

A deep pouch for storing poopy-scooping bags is made by knitting a full bag-sized pocket on the back of the existing bag. This pouch is worked in the round making double decreases at each corner before using a three-needle bind-off to seal the remaining opening at the center.

With pocket openings facing you, start at the Light Turquoise end of the bag and use the crochet hook and Avocado yarn to pick up and transfer stitches to the circular needle. Pick up 60 stitches along one side of the bag, 2 stitches in 1 stitch at the corner, 24 stitches along the bottom, 2 stitches in 1 stitch at the next corner and another 60 stitches along the other long side. Cast on 26 stitches to go across the top of the pouch. 174 stitches on needle. Join, being careful not to twist.

**First round:** The 2 stitches at each corner will be knit together, and the top of the bag is worked in Seed Stitch: K60, k2tog, k24, k2tog, k59, k2tog, [K1, p1] 12 times, k2tog.

**Second Round:** Knit until 1 stitch before your decreased stitch at the corner, sl 1, k2tog, psso. Do the same at the remaining 3 corners, maintaining Seed Stitch at top end.

**Subsequent rounds:** Maintain Seed Stitch top for 4 more rows then switch to Stockinette Stitch and Light Turquoise yarn. Continue double decreases in each corner. After 5 rounds of Light Turquoise, switch to Teal yarn. When top and bottom decreases meet in the middle, turn bag inside, out and divide stitches evenly on 2 needles (top decrease point to bottom decrease point). Use three-needle bind off to seal the center. Cut yarn.

## Straps

The straps are connected to the top of the bag at the sides where it folds. Starting 1.5 inches from the fold on one side, pick up 9 stitches from the pouch side and 9 stitches from the pockets side for a total of 18 stitches.

## Start Strap Stitch

Row 1: [Sl 1, k1] across,
Row 2: Sl 1 stitch, then k across. Repeat these 2 rows.

Continue Strap Stitch for 12 inches. Then k2tog at the beginning of each row until 1 stitch remains. Pull yarn through last stitch for a nice pointy end.

Pick up and knit a second strap on the other side. Make it at least 36-inches long, depending on how low you want the bag to hang. Remember, the strap will stretch a bit. Run the longer strap through both square rings, fold over 2 inches, and capture the rings on the loop: 4 inches from active end, pick up 1 stitch from the strap and k2tog with 1 stitch from needle. Repeat for all stitches. Bind off.

### FINISHING

## Pocket opening border

On the first pocket, use Avocado yarn and pick up 17 live stitches from the bottom of the waste yarn openings and 1 extra from each side for a total of 19 stitches. Seed Stitch 1 row. Pick up the 17 live stitches plus 2 end stitches along the top of the opening. Bind off the stitches along top edge of pocket opening. Continue working back and forth in Seed Stitch for 5 rows. Bind off in pattern.

Make borders as above for the remaining two pockets using Teal yarn on Avocado section and Light Turquoise on Teal section.

Using the tail ends of the borders, Whipstitch the sides of each border to the pouch, starting at the sealing rows just above the openings. Weave in ends. Steam lightly.

# "Get Along Little Doggy" Saddlebag

*By Amy Swenson*

While we don't recommend using fido as a mule, this lightweight pouch allows your pooch to carry house keys, a change purse, and the all-important plastic bags for picking up poop. Let him wear it at home before you hit the streets; he may freeze (or buck) until he gets used to the feel. But he should warm to it soon enough—dogs love to help their masters, after all.

## MATERIALS

* Schoeller Stahl Big Mexico (100% superwash wool; 85 m per 50g skein); Color: 7955 (Sombrero); 2(3, 4) skeins

* 1 set US 4/3.5 mm needles (or size needed to match gauge)

* 1-inch wide Velcro strip, approximately 3-inches long

## GAUGE

24 stitches/32 rows = 4 inches in Stockinette Stitch

(For substitutions, look for a yarn with a recommended gauge of approximately 19 stitches/ 28 rows = 4 inches on US 7/4.5 mm needles)

## SIZE

**Pouch to pouch:** 14(17, 21) inches
**Width:** 5(6, 7) inches
**Pouch depth:** 4(5, 6) inches

## BAG

Cast on 30(36, 42) stitches.

### First Pocket

Work 6 rows in Garter Stitch (knit all rows).
Switch to Stockinette Stitch and continue until piece measures 4(5, 6) inches from cast on edge, ending with a RS row.
Turn work and k across this WS row.
Purl next RS row. Continue in Reverse Stockinette Stitch until piece measures 8(10, 12) inches from cast on edge, ending with a RS row.

### Back Piece

Beginning on next WS row, work back piece as follows:
Next row: K4, p to last 4 stitches, k4.
Next row: Knit.

Repeat these two rows until piece measures 14(17, 21) inches from cast on edge, ending with a WS row.

## Second Pocket

Continue in Stockinette Stitch (without Garter Stitch edge) until piece measures 18(22, 27) inches from cast on edge, ending with a RS row. Turn work and continue in Reverse Stockinette Stitch until piece measures 21.5(26.5, 33.5) inches. Work 6 rows in Garter Stitch. Bind off all stitches.

## Belly Straps

(make two)
Cast on 24(30, 36) stitches. Work in Garter Stitch for 14 rows. Bind off.

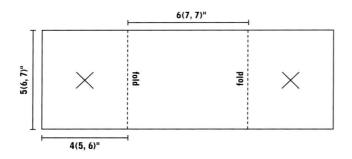

6(7, 7)"

5(6, 7)"

fold

fold

4(5, 6)"

**Attach straps at X on underside of bag**

strap — velcro

### FINISHING

Fold in pockets in half, and sew side seams. Attach belly straps to underside of saddle bags, approximately 3 inches from the bottom of pouch. Sew Velcro strip to underside of belly straps with sewing needle and thread so that fasteners will attach to one another without twisting the strap.

# Disco Dog Legwarmers

*By Kristi Porter*

A coat (his own or one you've knit!) keeps a dog's body warm, but often his legs are left out in the cold. For older dogs, or those who suffer from arthritis or other joint pain, keeping their legs warm is an act of kindness. For all dogs, this quartet of legwarmers, knit in a fabulous hand-dyed superwash wool from **Curious Creek Fibers**, will bring warmth and lots of laughs to a cold, damp day.

## MATERIALS

* Curious Creek Fibers Serengeti (100% superwash wool; 123 yds per 50g skein):
  [MC] Color: Anemone; 2(2, 3) skeins
  [CC] Color: Sunrise on Daffodils; 1 skein

* 1 set US 4/3.5 mm DPNs
* 1 set US 2/2.75 mm DPNs
(or size needed to match gauge)

* K1C2 Rainbow Elastic 1 mm (cotton wrapped latex core; 50 yds per card); Color: 64 Violet; 1 card

## GAUGE

24 stitches/32 rows = 4 inches over Stockinette Stitch on US 4 needles

## SIZE

**Foreleg Warmers**
**Ankle:** 3.25(4.5, 5.5) inches
**Above Knee:** 4.25(7, 8) inches
**Length** (with 2 inches of ribbing doubled at either end): 5(7, 9) inches

**Hindleg Warmers**
**Ankle:** 3.25(4, 4.5) inches
**Above Knee:** 6.5(10, 14) inches
**Length** (with 2 inches of ribbing doubled at either end): 7(9, 11) inches

## FORELEG WARMERS

Cast on 20(28, 32) stitches on smaller needles with MC. Distribute stitches evenly over needles. Place marker and join to begin in the round. Work around in k2, p2 rib for 4 inches. Switch to larger needles, continue in rib as established, and work a 1-inch stripe with CC. Alternate 1-inch stripes in CC and MC. At the same time, increase as follows:

After 2nd stripe (when legwarmer measures 5 inches): Continue in MC and *k1, m1, k1, p2* around.

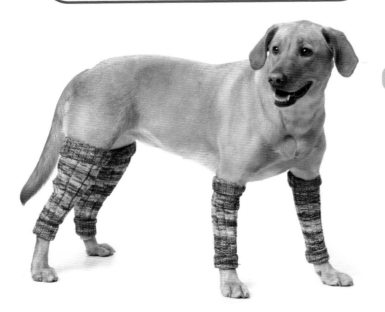

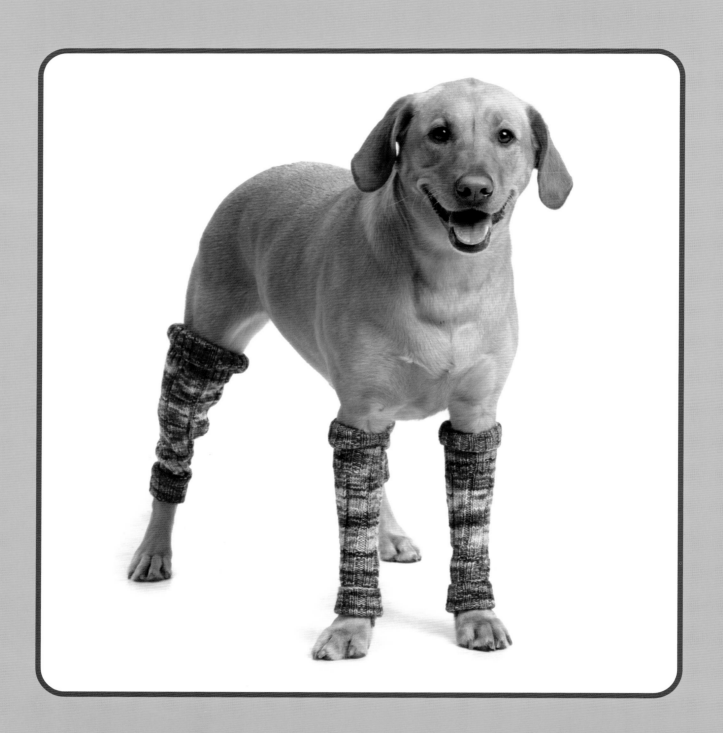

**Size S only:** Switch back to smaller needles and break off CC. Work 4 inches in k3, p2 rib (without stripes). Bind off all 25 stitches in rib.

**Size M and L:** Continue in k3, p2 rib on larger needles.

After 4th stripe (when legwarmer measures 7 inches): Continue in MC and *k1, m1, k2, p2* around.

**For Size M only:** Switch back to smaller needles and break off CC. Work 4 inches in k2, p2 rib (without stripes). Bind off 42 stitches in rib.

**Size L:** Continue in k4, p2 rib.

When legwarmer measures 9 inches make final stripe and switch back to smaller needles. Break off CC. Work in k2, p2 rib for 4 inches (without stripes) and bind off 48 stitches in rib.

## HINDLEG WARMERS

**Note:** For all sizes, use Rainbow Elastic in a color that matches your yarn (or is slightly darker) carried along with the MC during the final 2 inches of ribbing to help keep the legwarmers from slipping down. Drop the elastic and weave in before binding off.

With MC and smaller needles cast on 20(24, 28) stitches with smaller needles. Place marker and join in the round. Work in k2, p2 rib for 4 inches.

Switch to larger needles. Work a 1-inch stripe in CC. Continue alternating stripes every inch until you return to smaller needles. At the same time, work increases as follows in each row following a stripe.
After 1st stripe: *K1, m1, k1, p2* around and continue in k3, p2 rib.
After 2nd stripe: *K1, m1, k2, p2* around and continue in k4, p2 rib.

After 3rd stripe: *K1, m1, k3, p2* around and continue in k5, p2 rib.
After 4th stripe: *K1, m1, k4, p2* around.

**Size S only:** Switch back to smaller needles, break off CC, and work in k2, p2 rib (without stripes) for 4 inches. Bind off in rib.

**Size M and L:** Continue in k6, p2 rib on larger needles.
After 5th stripe: *K1, m1, k5, p2* around and continue in k7, p2 rib.
After 6th stripe: *K1, m1, k6, p2* around.

**Size M only:** Switch back to smaller needles, break off CC, and work in k2, p2 rib (without stripes) for 4 inches. Bind off in rib.

**Size L:** Continue in k8, p2 rib on larger needles.
After 7th stripe: *K1, m1, k7, p2* around and continue in k9, p2 rib.
After 8th stripe: *K1, m1, k8, p2* around. (84 stitches)

Next row: Switch to smaller needles, break off CC, and continue in k2, p2 rib for 4 inches. Bind off in rib.

Weave in all ends. Fold over the top and bottom ribbing 2 inches to help keep the legwarmers in place when the dog is wearing them.

# Meet the Dogs

Sweetpea

Romeo

Belle and Max

Walter

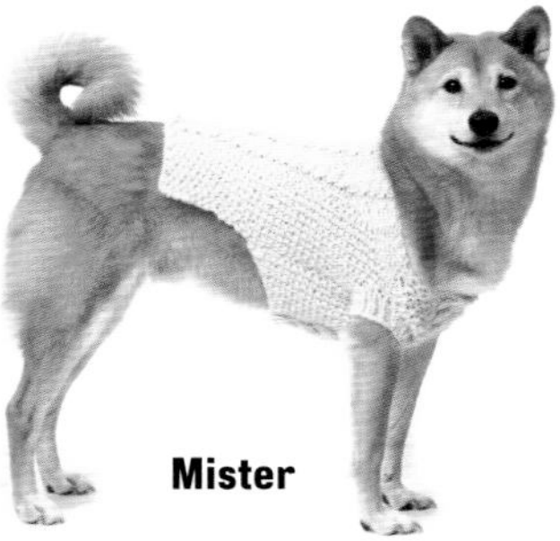

Mister

Eli

Chloe

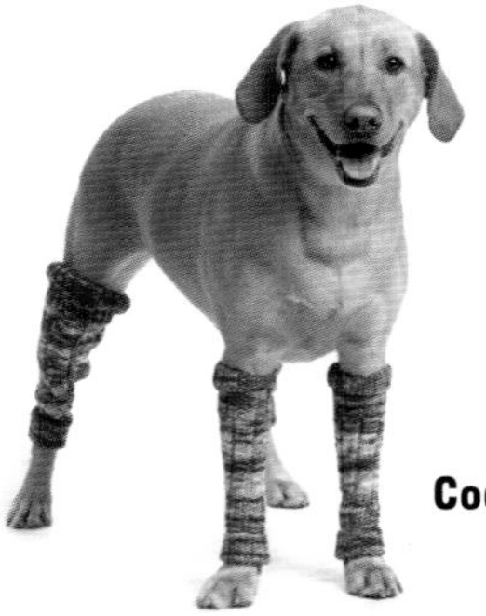

Cody

Toby

Willie

Foxy

Maxi and Belle

Rev

Connor

Raleigh

Madge

Huey

Lola

Pico and Luca

Rocco and Bella

Murphy

Coco

# About the Designers

**Staceyjoy Elkin** is the owner of Red Lipstick, a boutique in Brooklyn, New York, that sells handmade knitwear and other unique clothing. She has designed custom knitwear for Madonna and Sigourney Weaver, and worked for Donna Karan and Calvin Klein. She made her first dog sweater for her Chihuahua, Wylie.

**Amy Swenson** contributed designs to *Stitch 'n Bitch Nation* and *Knit Wit*, and her work appears regularly online at knitty.com. She lives in Calgary, Alberta, but IndiKnits, a line of her original patterns, can be found in yarn shops across North America. She doubts her four cats will forgive her for participating in this project, but intends to try to make it up to them with lots of treats. For additional information about her knitwear, visit www.indiknits.com.

**Kristi Porter** is a knitwear designer, technical editor, teacher, and author, whose work has been featured in *Knit Wit* and the Knitgrrl series. She is the designer for Curious Creek Fibers (www.curiouscreek.com) and has appeared on the DIY television series *Knitty Gritty*. A regular contributor of features and patterns to knitty.com, Kristi has been involved with this online magazine since its inception.

Kristi doesn't remember who taught her to knit as a kid, though it's likely her granny, Aunt Bricky, and mother, Judy, would all be willing to take credit. She was a designer as soon as she learned the basics, creating patterns from a few hastily taken measurements and a vague idea of the architecture of the garment. She still loves a design challenge, whether for people or animals. She lives with her husband, Leo, daughters, Zoe and Eleanor, a cat and two sock dogs in La Jolla, California.

**Heather Brack** is a knitter and writer in Cleveland, Ohio. Her shih tzu, Black Francis, will curl up and nap on top of anything handknit, but he especially loves receiving handmade sweaters. Heather's work appears in the Knitgrrl book series by Shannon Okey (www.knitgrrl.com). She also self-publishes a line of knitting patterns under the name Beeline.

**Kate Watson** tries to hide from her growing reputation as a knitting numbers geek, but has to admit that she enjoys the technical aspects of knitwear design. Her work appears in *Knit Wit*. In the winter, she's torn between loving her hometown of Toronto and despairing over her ancestors' decision that Canada is The Place to Be.

# Resources

## YARN SOURCES

Artful Yarns
*www.jcacrafts.com*

Berroco
*www.berroco.com*

Brown Sheep
*www.brownsheep.com*

Cascade
*www.cascadeyarns.com*

Crystal Palace & Ashford Yarns
*www.straw.com*

Curious Creek Fibers
*www.curiouscreek.com*

Karabella
*www.karabellayarns.com*

Lang
*www.langyarns.ch*

Lion Brand
*www.lionbrand.com*

Mission Falls
In the U.S., contact Unique Kolours
*www.uniquekolours.com*
In Canada contact Mission Falls
*www.missionfalls.com*

Noro
In the U.S., contact Knitting Fever, Inc.
*http://knittingfever.com*

OnLine
In the U.S., contact Knitting Fever, Inc.
*http://knittingfever.com*

Schachenmayr
In the U.S. contact Knitting Fever, Inc
*www.knittingfever.com*

Schoeller + Stahl
*www.schoeller-und-stahl.de*

Tahki –Stacy Charles, Inc
*www.tahkistacycharles.com*

## SQUEAKERS
*www.dogtoys.com/justsqueakers.html*

## SOME GOOD BOOKS...
These handy books will teach you
knitting basics, refresh your skills, or
help you master new techniques.

Melville, Sally. *The Knit Stitch: The
Knitting Experience, Book 1, and The
Purl Stitch: The Knitting Experience,
Book 2*, XRX Books, Sioux Falls, SD:
2002 and 2003.

Singer, Amy R. *Knit Wit: 30 Easy
and Hip Projects*. New York:
HarperCollins, 2004.

Stoller, Debbie. *Stitch 'n Bitch:
The Knitter's Handbook*. New York:
Workman Publishing, 2000.

*Vogue Knitting: The Ultimate Knitting
Book*. New York: Sixth&Spring
Books, 2002, originally published
by Pantheon, 1989.

*Vogue Knitting Quick Reference:
The Ultimate Portable Knitting
Compendium*, New York:
Sixth&Spring Books, 2002.

## AND HELPFUL WEBSITES
These online resources will expand
your knitting horizons—and they're
a great help when you're trying to
figure out how to k2tog tbl in the
middle of the night!

*www.knitting.about.com*
*www.learntoknit.com*
*www.vogueknitting.com/tech/tech.html*
*www.knitty.com*

# Index